Becoming Brave

Winning Marriage Equality in Oklahoma and Finding Our Voice

To Deb –

Always be brave!
Sharon Bishop-Baldwin
& Mary Bishop-Baldwin

BY SHARON BISHOP-BALDWIN
with MARY BISHOP-BALDWIN

Shmaryon Publications
Broken Arrow, Oklahoma

For the greatest dream team ever –
Sue and Gay, Don and Kay,
James, Joe and Jeff.

For Toby, our brother in arms.

For my favorite sister, Jan,
our greatest cheerleader.

For Mary, without whom
absolutely none of this
would have happened.
I love you most.

CONTENTS

PREFACE

I've always enjoyed writing. As a high school student, I was a little abnormally gleeful about essay assignments, and once I settled on journalism as my major in college, I thrived on churning out copy – feature stories, hard-news stories … it didn't matter, as long as I was writing.

When I began my editing career on the Tulsa World's copy desk in 1993 and stayed there for nearly 21 years, I had to search a little harder for writing assignments, but taking a turn at the occasional Monday column or a travel piece based on our most recent vacation, in addition to crafting Mary's and my annual Christmas letter, usually satisfied the need.

In all those years, though, I never imagined that I would write a book. Of course, for most of my life, I also never imagined I would be a plaintiff in a federal civil-rights lawsuit that would end at the United States Supreme Court. Life is full of unexpected journeys.

The journey described in this book is the sort of

epic adventure that makes a person say, "Well, I can die now, because it will never get better than that." I'm nowhere near ready to take that *final* journey, but it is true that I can't fathom anything that will ever happen in my life being more fulfilling, more exciting or more incredible than being a standard-bearer in the fight for marriage equality in Oklahoma.

Because of a lawsuit Mary and I and another couple, Gay and Sue, filed a dozen years ago, we have met world leaders, helped educate law school students and high school students, and have been celebrated and feted beyond our wildest dreams. But the greatest gift of our decade-long fight for marriage equality was getting to be a champion for a group of people who needed one.

It has truly been the honor of our lives to represent you in working for and reaching a goal that has changed the world for the better for so many people. Know, though, that in changing the world, we have been changed more.

Your love and support kept our collective dream afloat. When we were exhausted, you energized us. When we were discouraged, you made us hopeful. When we were worried, your belief in us made us defiant. And when we celebrated, you cheered right alongside us.

Never think that each of you didn't help make marriage equality the law of the land in Oklahoma and the United States. You did.

The thing that worries me the most about this book is that I might have gotten something wrong.

Although I understand a lot more about the law than a lot of lay people, thanks to a 10-year lawsuit, I'm still not a lawyer. I have worked hard to get it right, but I'm human. Any errors of fact are solely mine.

Any errors of grammar are solely my editor's. Just kidding. I am immensely fortunate to be married to the greatest editor of all time, and she edited this book for free, so I'll also claim the grammatical slips. Mary, I love you beyond measure for so many reasons; being my editor in chief is just one of them.

The thing that most breaks my heart about this book is that not all of you will see your names in it. I have elected not to write an acknowledgments section because there's simply not enough ink in the world to tell all of you just how much you mean to me and us.

The people who are named herein were integral to the stories we chose to tell. There were stories we decided not to tell for one reason or another, and it might be that had we told different stories, your name would have appeared. Please know that the presence or lack of your name in print in this book is no measure of what your friendship means to us.

Thanks in advance for reading. And thanks a million times for being the best – and probably the biggest – extended family a couple of bullheaded Oklahoma social justice fighters could ever hope to have. We love you more than you can imagine.

CHAPTER ONE:
THE RULING

We were running late for work, as usual. Three minutes before the start of a daily story meeting at the Tulsa World, where we both worked as editors, we were parking the car outside the building. My cellphone started buzzing. It said the caller was Toby Jenkins, the executive director of Oklahomans for Equality. Toby is one of our best friends, and phone conversations with him are sometimes lengthy.

"It's Toby," I said, getting out of the car and reaching into the back seat for our lunch bag. "And I do *not* have time to talk to him now. We can call him after the meeting."

The call went to voicemail, and the phone started ringing again almost immediately.

"It's Toby again," I said. "Whatever it is, it's just going to have to wait."

Mary and I made a mad dash into the building, relieved to see all the editors still milling about. Most people get annoyed by meetings that start late, but as a second-shift worker whose day started every day with that meeting, I can tell you that those delays are sometimes a saving grace.

I sat down at my computer to log on, and Mary did the same. City Editor Paul Tyrrell walked by my desk and said casually, "You need to check Pacer."

Pacer is a website on which federal court decisions are filed. It's a wonderful resource for reporters who are trying to track the progress of federal court cases. Thing is, I wasn't a reporter. I was a copy editor. I didn't use Pacer. Didn't know how. Didn't even have a log-in.

There was only one reason in the entire world that Paul would be telling me, a plaintiff in a nearly decade-old federal lawsuit challenging Oklahoma's constitutional ban on same-sex marriage, to "check Pacer."

My heart stopped.

"Do we have a ruling?" I asked him.

Doing his best to avoid eye contact, Paul shrugged his shoulders. "Just check it," he said, walking away.

"Paul! Do we have a ruling?" I practically shouted, carefully enunciating each syllable as though he had suddenly stopped comprehending English.

He ignored me. He told me later that he didn't think it was right that I should hear that news from the city editor and that he was trying to extricate himself from the moment.

I told him that he had long been one of my best friends in the newsroom and that there were few people more appropriate to share that news with me. But in that moment, all I knew was that he was inexplicably blowing me off.

I ran to Mary's desk, and she said she knew that something was up but not what. So we headed to the desk of David Harper, the Tulsa World's federal court reporter at the time.

Mary got there first, and I looked up in time to see her peering over David's shoulder at his computer screen, her palms pressed together over her nose and mouth. I reached her side in time to hear David saying in the calmest, coolest voice: "Well, let's see here, ... it's 68 pages ... ."

Mary was all but hyperventilating when David, wisely surmising that he needed to jump straight to the end, got to page 67, where U.S. District Judge Terence C. Kern of the Tulsa-based Northern District of Oklahoma had written:

"The Court declares that Part A of the Oklahoma Constitutional Amendment violates the Equal Protection Clause of the Fourteenth Amendment to the U.S. Constitution."

Mary turned to me, a look of complete and utter shock on her face, and said, almost in a whisper, "We won."

Tears fell, embarrassingly, as we embraced then and there in the crowded newsroom, our co-workers looking on, trying to discern whether the news was good or bad.

"We won!" I shouted, and there was a riffle of

Tulsa World reporter Jarrel Wade snapped this photo with his iPhone just as Mary – looking over the shoulder of then-federal court reporter David Harper – was discovering that Tulsa federal Judge Terence Kern had ruled in our favor on Jan. 14, 2014. Courtesy/Jarrel Wade

applause as many of our colleagues made their way to us to offer congratulations and hugs.

As Mary and I continued to hold each other, I was keenly aware that we were seriously overstepping the bounds of professional conduct, something we'd always been so cautious about since the earliest days of our newsroom romance.

I also became acutely aware at some point that then-Photo Editor Christopher Smith was circling us, camera in hand, clicking away like we were supermodels at a photo shoot.

As newspaper editors, both of us for more than

20 years, we know a news story when we see one. But it wasn't until that moment that I began to realize fully the gravity of what had just happened and how our lives were about to change. The next half-hour was a blur. For reasons that aren't at all obvious today, I went to that meeting we had been running late for. I think I was trying to maintain some semblance of normalcy, but surrealism was ruling the day as I sat there listening to other editors discuss a recent spate of careless typos.

As a proud grammarian, I'm *always* up for talking about misplaced modifiers and sloppy spelling, but on that day, I just couldn't do it. My heart wasn't in it. I wanted to scream! I wanted to run away! And when my phone buzzed mid-meeting and I looked down to see that it was our lead attorney calling, I did just that. I stood up and left without a word. I hope – and believe – I've been forgiven.

Mary, who never even went to the meeting, was sitting at her desk, already deep into her talking points with an Associated Press reporter who had called. We then talked to our lead attorney, Don Holladay, briefly and promised to celebrate and strategize together soon.

Then, we finally called Toby. After a few shared screams of elation, we told him we were going to the house so I could change shirts, that the one I had worn that day wasn't particularly flattering, and then we'd come to the Equality Center.

"But the cameras are already here," he protested. "You need to come here."

Fine, we agreed. We'll go there for a quick word or two, and then we'll go home and change. We would be back in time for an evening rally that, at that moment, was about 10 minutes into the planning stages.

Indeed, several news trucks were already set up outside the Dennis R. Neill Equality Center just blocks from the newspaper office downtown.

The ruling wasn't yet an hour old, but we'd have been hard-pressed to find anyone around who didn't know about it.

Equally shocking was the number of people who apparently wanted to talk to us about it. For career news women, being the news makers was unfamiliar territory.

A first round of interviews went by at dizzying speed. Between on-camera remarks with all of the local network affiliates, we did several quick telephone interviews with reporters from the country's largest newspapers.

Stolen glances at my phone told me I would be exceeding my text-message limit that night and that my Facebook was going to short-circuit.

And through it all, I kept thinking about that shirt, the one I wanted to change so badly. So when we had a second to catch our breath, I said to Mary, "Let's run home so I can change shirts."

The TV reporter to whom we had just promised a live tease at the top of the next broadcast in less than an hour turned pale. "You don't have time!" he cried. "I've been to your house. There's no way!"

Judge strikes Oklahoma same-sex marriage ban

TOP STORIES   January 14, 2014 6:29 PM EST

PHOTO: A federal court Tuesday ruled that Oklahoma law limiting marriage to one man and one woman violates the U.S. Constitution.

Judge Kern's ruling was a top story on CNN, this screen shot from a friend's phone shows. The background photo was shot by our friend and videographer Eric Turner, who had his own 15 minutes of fame as a result of its widespread use.

Courtesy

"Oh, sure," we said. "We'll be quick. We'll drive home, change, and be right back. We won't miss a thing."

The reporter and Toby were both looking at us without saying a word, clearly doing their best not to tell the plaintiffs who had just overturned the state ban on same-sex marriage that we were idiots, but it was obvious in their faces.

"We promise," we insisted one last time before rushing out the door to the car.

As editors who had worked the second shift for roughly two decades, we had often boasted that we knew little of the phenomenon called rush-hour traffic. When we were typically headed into downtown, everyone else was outbound. When we were outbound, at midnight, everyone else was in bed.

So when we got on the highway entrance ramp for our "quick" trip home to change a shirt, our chins hit the floorboard. Where did all these cars come from? The Broken Arrow Expressway was a parking lot!

We weren't going home; that much was obvious. Mary steered to the first exit and headed for Utica Square, an upscale shopping center that was our closest option.

At that moment, my phone rang. It was a reporter for The Los Angeles Times. What followed must have looked like a comedy skit straight out of Hollywood.

As Mary pulled into a parking space outside Saks, I was still talking to the reporter. As we got out of the car, I kept talking and followed Mary's footsteps. Once in the store, I was still talking, yet I was vaguely aware of Mary's voice, clearly agitated, rising as she exclaimed to a clerk, "What do you *mean* you don't have plus sizes?"

Then, as quickly as we had walked in, we were walking out, with me still on the phone with the reporter, still following Mary's footsteps.

As we settled back into the car, I wrapped up the call – I don't think the reporter ever had an inkling of what was taking place on my end of the conversation – and Mary and I began to discuss our options.

Mary was convinced that the shirt I was wearing was fine. I was beginning to agree that it was going to *have* to be fine when I thought of Plan B: my sister.

Nine years older, my sister, Jan Baldwin, wears the same size I do and has similar tastes in clothes. Perfect. One quick phone call later, she was on her way to rendezvous with us at the Equality Center with five of my favorite shirts – of hers – in tow.

Much to the relief of quite a few local television reporters, Mary and I made the live teases at the top of the 6 p.m. newscasts. I changed into a borrowed shirt, and then the real festivities began.

The energy and joy we experienced at the Equality Center that night were beyond anything we had ever felt. *We won!* What an amazing, incredible thing to be a part of.

My sister has joked that she still hasn't gotten used to people standing and applauding when we walk into a room. "That's just Sharon and Mary!" she exclaims. I understand, because I feel that way, too. Although we have felt the love and gratitude of Tulsa's LGBT community for a number of years now, the response that night was beyond description.

The thing that is always at the back of our minds, though, is that this isn't about us per se. The response is not because Sharon and Mary are such great gals (although we like to think that we're pretty friendly); it's because *someone* in this reddest of the red states did *something* that made a dent in the anti-gay bigotry that seemed so pervasive in Oklahoma.

It is that rare accomplishment that landed us on MSNBC for a live interview less than 24 hours after Judge Kern's ruling was handed down.

Perhaps it was the lack of sleep – we literally napped from 7 to 8 that Wednesday morning, having spent the entire night trying to catch up on emails and Facebook messages and notifications, read every news story we could find about the ruling, make the arrangements with an MSNBC producer for the appearance and *read the actual ruling* – but every tiny ounce of television know-how we learned in those few short hours after the ruling came down had totally drained from our bodies.

We both wore print blouses – conflicting print blouses. We were exhausted and looked like it. We were hoarse. I wiffed a softball question.

The learning curve for media savviness is surprisingly steep, and we were behind it. It was and still is easily our worst interview. Even our kindest friends said, "Well, … you were tired."

We've had so many opportunities since then to do better, and we have. By now, we know our subject forward and backward. We know to wear solid colors, and not clashing ones. We take care of our voices and try to stay rested.

It's odd to think about these things, but it's like being the parent of a new baby – there's something greater than us, and we have to take care of it. For us, it's a cause. And if promoting our cause requires some life adjustment and learning on our parts, so be it.

In retrospect, I wish I hadn't worried so much about my silly shirt on the afternoon of the ruling. Few people remember what I wore anyway, and besides, it didn't compare to the horrors of the blouse I wore the following day during the MSNBC appearance.

There's nothing quite as surreal as seeing your own face on "The Daily Show." Jon Stewart's segment about marriage equality coming to Oklahoma was a huge hit among our friends and followers. Courtesy

And as luck would have it, a clip from *that* interview was the one comedian Jon Stewart used for his segment on "The Daily Show" about our marriage-equality victory in Oklahoma.

For the record, I am not the woman who knows exactly when and how many times she's worn each blouse in her closet.

I am not the woman who won't leave her house without her makeup being impeccable.

I certainly am not the woman who has face powder and blush, an extra tube of lipstick and a comb in her purse at all times.

Or at least I didn't used to be. Life has a funny way of changing a person, even if only temporarily.

I know that one of these days, I'll once again be "just Sharon," the woman who looks at a shirt in the closet and thinks, "Did I wear that two days ago?" I'll be the woman who doesn't waste a single brain cell thinking about whether my liquid foundation is a tad too dark for an early spring day.

I look forward to that day. Being a plaintiff in a lawsuit that has gained national and even worldwide attention has certainly been a wild ride, but especially once Judge Kern's ruling came in, the pace and demands on us were dizzying at times.

We half-joked that it was like having an unpaid part-time job – full time on occasion, it seemed – but there was more truth to it than maybe even we realized.

It hadn't always been that way, though. For the first nine years and two months after we filed the suit, few people – few reporters, few lawyers, few gay-rights activists and groups – even knew who we were.

CHAPTER TWO:
THE COMMITMENT CEREMONY

Like a lot of couples, Mary and I met at work. I started at the Tulsa World in August 1993, and Mary joined the staff just shy of two years later, in July 1995. By November 1996, I had moved in with her, and within just a few months, we had negotiated with our bosses to work the same shift on the same days in a cavernous newsroom where our desks were never more than 10 to 15 feet apart.

That much togetherness can be a real test of a relationship, I'm told, but we never felt a need to get away from each other. In fact, within a couple of years, we donated one of our two cars to charity because its tires were beginning to get brittle from lack of use. We haven't owned two vehicles since.

Although Mary and I both like romance and celebrate special occasions in memorable ways, the origins of our decision to have a commitment ceremony were embarrassingly unremarkable.

I know it would make a better story to say that I

got down on one knee and dramatically asked Mary to spend the rest of her life with me, but the truth is, we were just planning a vacation.

Jim Stanton, a longtime friend of Mary's from Rhode Island – they met during graduate school at Arkansas State University in the mid-1980s – wanted us all to take a beach trip together, so we began looking at rental houses in Florida.

We found a great little place on the Gulf Coast about an hour's drive south of Tallahassee, a spot in the road called Alligator Point, with a beach house for rent by a lesbian couple who for years had owned and operated the Naiad Press, a lesbian book publisher. It was perfect!

I don't recall exactly when and how the vacation became a commitment ceremony, but before long, we had two beach houses reserved and a minister lined up; nine additional friends and family members were planning to attend; and we were writing vows.

It seems funny to say all of this so matter-of-factly. The truth is, none of it was routine. We were in uncharted territory.

Although securing a minister was easy – a good friend was ordained in the Unitarian Universalist Church, which had affirmed the right of its clergy to officiate at holy unions as early as 1984 – garnering our family's support was not always so.

My father, Richard Baldwin, and his then-companion would attend happily, as would my sister. I had always been lucky that my family's love felt confidently secure.

At the risk of sounding anti-religious – I know that there are many people of faith who are not automatically opposed to homosexuality – I was fortunate that my father and sister were without the frequently seen religious hang-ups that can get in the way of otherwise good relationships.

But Mary's brother and sister-in-law decided that they could not condone our relationship by witnessing our vows. Their refusal to attend on religious grounds created a rift that exists still today.

We might have understood their reticence had there been a history of problems in our relationship with them, but for years we had spent occasional weekends together, with them staying at our house and their young daughters sleeping in the bedroom next to ours.

We had enjoyed concerts, attended ballgames and watched Fourth of July fireworks together, but somehow, for them, this was asking too much.

Likewise, Mary's mother and her second husband decided not to attend our commitment ceremony, although their decision was colored at least in part by health concerns.

Realizing that her family's love was conditional was understandably painful for Mary.

Over the years, her mother, Fern Peery, has made great progress regarding her acceptance of us and her understanding of LGBT issues as a whole, and we celebrate that change. But most of that progress has come *since* our commitment ceremony, not before.

And Mary's brother and sister-in-law and now-grown nieces have held fast to their church's teachings. They have rarely been in our home since our commitment-ceremony invitation. They have never spent the night since then. We rarely see them and only recently met Mary's 3-year-old great-niece and year-old great-nephew.

Although we don't often notice those family members' absence from our daily lives, we find it immensely sad that these rifts exist.

As difficult as a family member's rejection usually is, most LGBT people can also tell you horror stories about being refused service at a business or some similar slight, creating feelings of shame and embarrassment.

Although these incidents might not hurt our hearts as deeply as a family member's rejection, the effect on our self-esteem is real and cumulative. And it was with this backpack full of fear and potential rejection that we were about to embark on a very public display of affection across two states.

By today's standards, weddings for same-sex couples are routine, but such was not the case in Oklahoma in late 1999 and early 2000.

At a time when many gay men and lesbians in Oklahoma worried about being assaulted by strangers and felt emboldened by simply holding hands in public once a year at the Pride parade and festival – the ones who were out of the closet enough to attend at all, that is – we somehow never really thought of it as courageous to order pink and purple napkins embossed in silver with our names and wedding date from a local retailer.

And we were honored when our recently retired minister at the First Christian Church in Tulsa loaned us a chalice from his personal collection to use for Communion during our commitment ceremony.

But all of this was in Oklahoma, where at least we had a feel for the climate. What would the reception be like in Florida? Rural Florida, even.

To add complexity, we were planning this event from 1,000 miles away in the days before we had Internet service at home or even at our desks at work.

We did all of the leg work at "Internet stations" in the newsroom after our shift ended each night at midnight.

We ordered a wedding cake with the names of two women on it; we ordered flowers – two bridal bouquets and an arrangement for the cake table; we made dinner reservations for 10 people for the night before the ceremony, our "rehearsal dinner," of sorts; and we ordered food for our reception, all without so much as one refusal of service or even an awkward pause as the nature of our requests sunk in.

When we arrived at Forget Me Not Florist and Gifts in Crawfordville, Fla., a tiny town whose 2000 population was just 1,698, we found the woman with whom we had placed our order in the shop's back room, coaxing open the last Stargazer lily for our table arrangement so it would be just perfect for the ceremony.

Our commitment ceremony on March 26, 2000, at Alligator Point, Fla., was the closest thing we thought we would ever have to a wedding, and we planned the entire affair from 1,000 miles away.

Courtesy/
Jan Baldwin

She was clearly as attentive to our flowers as she would have been to those of any heterosexual couple.

Down the road at Myra Jean's Cakes, our interlocking hearts cake with purple wisteria and basketweave design on the sides was perfect, too. Myra Jean had made it herself and presented it to us, and she was so friendly and welcoming – just what you would expect of any Southern woman who makes cakes and pies for a living.

In the end, it didn't seem to matter at all, to anyone, that Mary and I were both women. That's not

Courtesy/Jan Baldwin

to say there weren't hitches – a dry cleaners employee in Tulsa brushed my unprotected dress up against the dirty car about 12 hours before our flight, so we had to find a cleaners in Tallahassee as soon as our plane touched down, and then it rained the evening of our ceremony, so our planned "sunset wedding on the beach" instead took place in the living room on sand-colored carpet.

But no heterosexual couple would have been immune to those glitches, and none of them really mattered, anyway. For us, this was all the "wedding" we thought we'd ever have.

We were surrounded by loved ones; we had great fun; and we formalized a commitment to each other that we had been feeling in our hearts for several years. Nothing else was required.

Or so we thought.

CHAPTER THREE:
THE GENESIS

Post-commitment ceremony life quickly settled into a comfortable routine of work and weekends, with the occasional vacation.

Like most young(ish) couples, we knew we needed to think about things such as estate planning, but it was not today's priority, not tomorrow's, not the next day's. Sometime in the fall of 2003, we decided to get serious about this adulthood stuff, so we found a lawyer, Tim Studebaker, and went to work.

Tim prepared a joint revocable trust plus individual wills, durable powers of attorney, living wills and health-care proxies. The grand total for all that legal work was $1,388.50, and that reflected a substantial "family" discount, which Tim gave LGBT clients at the time.

Although Tim's work and the documents were worth every penny, it wasn't lost on any of the three of us that for $50, a heterosexual couple could receive a marriage license that gave them all of the same protections plus many more. Thousands more benefits, in fact, many of which couldn't be purchased anywhere for any price without a marriage license.

It was as part of our casual discussion about this hypocrisy and inequity that the possibility of a lawsuit over Oklahoma's statutory ban on same-sex marriage arose.

Tim coincidentally attended a Law Day event at which he met Kay Bridger-Riley, a Tulsa lawyer whose firm was known for its civil rights practice, including employment discrimination cases.

In one case, Kay had represented a man who had been fired when his employer learned that he had AIDS, and his employer made that public. Kay sued for invasion of privacy and public disclosure of private facts but also filed a loss of consortium claim for the man's long-time partner.

Although the judge dismissed that claim, he actually apologized to the man's partner, explaining that he had to do so because there was no legal recognition of him as a spouse. Unfortunately, the client died the week before trial.

Kay had always had a lot of gay and lesbian clients, and at the time she was talking with Tim at the Law Day event, she had at least three gay or lesbian employees.

When Tim asked Kay what she thought about bringing a lawsuit to fight for marriage equality, she replied that she would love to take such a case – if only she had the right clients. Tim said he thought he could help her out.

The three of us – Tim, Mary and I – began scouring our contacts lists for other couples who might be willing to sign on to the suit. It was never our intention to go forward with such a small group of plaintiffs as we ultimately did, but you know what they say about going to war with the army you have.

Tim brought two couples from his church on board, and we three couples and Tim met in Kay's office one afternoon with some of her associates present, as well. Kay outlined where she thought the case would go, and then she and the other lawyers interviewed each couple privately, essentially to see what "skeletons" might be in those closets that the lawyers would have to contend with down the road.

One couple decided at that point not to continue as plaintiffs because one of them worked for a state institution. Suing the state probably wouldn't sit well with her employer, and she couldn't risk losing her job.

That left Mary and me and a couple we had just met but who would become like family over the course of the next decade and beyond – Sue Barton and Gay Phillips.

One of the great joys of our involvement with the fight for marriage equality has been our deep friendship with Sue and Gay. In many ways, it's a wonder that we ever got to know each other beyond those talks in the lawyer's office, though.

Gay and Sue are smokers, and Mary and I are bothered by cigarette smoke. Mary and I have a houseful of cats, and they're more dog people, plus

Sue is allergic to cats. They're both loyal Oklahoma State University fans, and, as an alumnus of the University of Oklahoma, I'm Sooner born and Sooner bred. Because of their jobs in the social work consulting field, they traveled a lot. Because of our jobs at a newspaper, we worked in the evenings.

It's nothing short of a miracle that such an abiding bond formed, but that's what happens when you have a common cause.

And then, when one couple's house burns down, as Sue and Gay's did, it seems only natural to help in every way possible, including having them over for our family Thanksgiving dinner only days later, on a day when Bedlam – the annual in-state rivalry football game between the University of Oklahoma and Oklahoma State University – just happened to be taking place. And it has seemed only natural several times since then to have Sue and Gay over to watch Bedlam at our place, even though they wear that hideous orange.

All joking aside, though, for the purposes of the lawsuit, it was, indeed, what set Mary and me *apart* from Gay and Sue that brought us all to the table to form what we hoped would be an unbeatable partnership.

Although Mary and I were not legally married anywhere, Gay and Sue had obtained a civil union in Vermont in August 2001, and before long, they would have a marriage license from Canada (May 2005) and another from California (November 2008).

It was this different approach that formed the basis of our two-pronged lawsuit. Mary and I were suing the state of Oklahoma for the right to marry in Oklahoma. Gay and Sue were suing Oklahoma to have their Vermont civil union (and later their Canadian and California marriage licenses) recognized by the state of Oklahoma.

And both couples were suing the federal government over the same points in relation to the Defense of Marriage Act. That would prove sticky for Mary and me later on, but at the beginning, that was the plan.

Our defendants were Oklahoma Gov. Brad Henry and state Attorney General Drew Edmondson, as well as President George W. Bush and U.S. Attorney General John Ashcroft.

It bothered Mary and me to sue Oklahoma's governor and attorney general. Both Democrats, they were rumored to be at least somewhat sympathetic to our cause, and we knew that they were just doing their jobs in enforcing the laws on the books. But we, too, had a "job" to do.

Ironically enough, one of Kay's first actions as our attorney of record was to consult with Tulsa County Court Clerk Sally Howe Smith, who ultimately became our defendant, about whether Mary and I needed to apply for a marriage license – fully understanding that we'd be turned down if we did.

Kay decided that we probably did not need to do so, a decision that later was walked back. But there were no precedents back then, no similar cases to use as an example. We were in uncharted waters right out here in the middle of the country.

Still, as alone as we often felt, we caught occasional glimpses of kindred spirits. We could see what was going on in the world around us as our lawsuit was taking shape in the spring of 2004.

In January of that year, President Bush, running for re-election on a strong pro-war platform in the wake of the 9/11 terror attacks, gave a State of the Union speech in which he essentially called for the U.S. Constitution to be amended to include a ban on same-sex marriages.

Nearly half of the 5,200-word speech was devoted to military efforts in Iraq and Afghanistan, but the president spent about 230 words discussing the importance of protecting the country's children from "the negative influence of the culture."

Bush said:

"Decisions children now make can affect their health and character for the rest of their lives. All of us – parents and schools and government – must work together to counter the negative influence of the culture and to send the right messages to our children.

"A strong America must also value the institution of marriage. I believe we should respect individuals as we take a principled stand for one of the most fundamental, enduring institutions of our civilization.

"Congress has already taken a stand on this issue by passing the Defense of Marriage Act, signed in

1996 by President Clinton. That statute protects marriage under federal law as the union of a man and a woman and declares that one state may not redefine marriage for other states.

"Activist judges, however, have begun redefining marriage by court order, without regard for the will of the people and their elected representatives. On an issue of such great consequence, the people's voice must be heard. If judges insist on forcing their arbitrary will upon the people, the only alternative left to the people would be the constitutional process. Our nation must defend the sanctity of marriage."

The president of the United States had just called on Congress and the citizens to thwart the judiciary in its legally mandated efforts to protect a minority population by urging that the U.S. Constitution be amended to include blatant, religion-based discrimination.

"If judges insist on forcing their arbitrary will upon the people, the only alternative left to the people would be the constitutional process. Our nation must defend the sanctity of marriage."

What President Bush was asking for was a fight. And one was certainly brewing.

CHAPTER FOUR:
THE IMPETUS

Actually, the fight for marriage equality had been brewing for some time.

Seven same-sex couples had filed a lawsuit in Massachusetts state court in April 2001 – in a case titled *Goodridge v. Department of Public Health* – asserting that the state marriage statute treated same-sex couples unequally.

Massachusetts' highest court, the Supreme Judicial Court, had declared in November 2003 that the state ban on same-sex marriages violated the state's constitution, but rather than simply opening up marriages to same-sex couples, the court stayed its ruling for six months and put the onus for resolving the situation on the Massachusetts Legislature.

State lawmakers had already been dealing with a proposed "Protection of Marriage Amendment" since July 2001, and similar legislation had been proposed as early as 1998.

A month later, in December 2003, the Massachusetts Senate submitted to the Supreme Judicial Court legislative language creating civil unions for same-sex couples and asked whether it satisfied the court's requirements in its *Goodridge* decision.

The court replied in February 2004 that the distinction between marriage and civil unions amounted to unconstitutional discrimination, even if the rights and obligations of each were identical.

The court reiterated that its stay had been intended to give the Legislature time to modify the state's marital laws to conform to its *Goodridge* decision – not to find a shortcut – and that had not been done.

Massachusetts lawmakers and then-Gov. Mitt Romney spent much of the spring of 2004 attempting to delay the impending lifting of the ban on same-sex marriages in the state. They wanted to get a proposed state constitutional ban on same-sex marriage before voters, and they argued that Massachusetts' lengthy constitutional convention process made a delay feasible.

Ultimately, their arguments fizzled, and the first legal marriage license issued to a same-sex couple in the United States – at least one that withstood court challenges – was handed out just after 12:01 a.m. on May 17, 2004, in Cambridge, Mass., to a lesbian couple, Marcia Hams and Susan Shepherd.

In all, more than 260 same-sex couples obtained marriage licenses that first night, surrounded by throngs of well-wishers sipping sparkling cider and eating wedding cake in a courthouse decked out just for the occasion.

But the spring of 2004 wasn't a pivotal time for

marriage equality on the East Coast alone. In California, the city of San Francisco had a new mayor, Gavin Newsom, who had been sworn in to office on Jan. 3.

Just 17 days later, Newsom was in Washington at the invitation of House Minority Leader Nancy Pelosi, whose congressional district encompasses most of the city and county of San Francisco, to attend President Bush's State of the Union address.

Newsom recalled, for Mother Jones magazine in a story published online on June 26, 2015, having heard the president's pronouncement supporting a constitutional amendment to ban same-sex marriage.

"Afterward, I was going back to get my cell phone, and a couple was standing right next to me in line and they were celebrating the president's speech," Newsom said.

"I remember it like it was yesterday — the way one of the two referred to the 'homosexual agenda.' They were so proud that the president was finally going to 'fix' that. And it was the way they said 'homosexual' that really struck a chord to me.

"Rather than walking downstairs to participate in a reception with Nancy Pelosi, I literally walked outside the Capitol and picked up my phone and called my staff and said, 'We need to do something about it.' "

What they did was start issuing marriage licenses.

Newsom directed the San Francisco County Clerk's Office to begin issuing marriage licenses to same-sex couples beginning Feb. 12. While critics said his order violated California state law, the mayor asserted that the state constitution's equal protection clause gave him that authority.

City officials reported issuing more than 900 licenses in the first three days.

Unlike in Massachusetts, which would grant marriage licenses only to same-sex couples who resided in Massachusetts or in another jurisdiction where same-sex marriages were legal, in California, all comers were welcome.

And come they did, in droves.

So many same-sex couples wanted San Francisco marriage licenses, in fact, that it quickly became obvious that a "first-come, first-served" method of application and distribution was not going to work, so couples were asked to make appointments. Even so, the lines reportedly stretched around the block from the office's opening each day until it closed each evening.

Here in Oklahoma, Mary and I were so touched by Gavin Newsom's stand for justice that we sent him and his clerk's office flowers!

That was a weird thing to do, perhaps, but we were reading news stories about supporters across the country calling San Francisco florists and paying for bouquets to be delivered to "any couple" in line, and we just thought it was unfair that the man who had started it all and the clerks who were doing all the work weren't getting any of the love.

Imagine our surprise when the mayor wrote us a personal thank-you note!

But with the fourth anniversary of our commitment ceremony coming up, it also seemed like a good time to get in on the act, so we made an appointment to get a marriage license in San Francisco on our anniversary, March 26, 2004.

We had no idea then how important it could have been for our future that we not keep that appointment; had we legally married in California, we could have put ourselves in the same classification as Sue and Gay – suing for the right of marital recognition, as opposed to suing for the right to marry.

Ultimately, California's Proposition 8 overturned those marriages, anyway.

Two weeks shy of our anniversary, on March 11, the California Supreme Court ordered Newsom and his clerks to halt issuing marriage licenses in violation of the current California statutes, and Newsom acquiesced.

Just five months later, the California high court declared the licenses that had been issued in that monthlong period and any marriages resulting from them to be void.

That included the first license that had been issued, to Phyllis Lyon and Del Martin. Lyon, then 79, and Martin, then 82, had been a couple for more than 50 years and had founded the Daughters of Bilitis, the first lesbian-rights group in the United States.

Although Phyllis and Del – we didn't know them; we just felt like we did – were our heroes, it was another couple who married in San Francisco County during that window who really caught our attention.

The marriage of San Francisco Chronicle City Hall reporter Rachel Gordon and Chronicle staff photographer Liz Mangelsdorf hardly made news anywhere outside the city by the bay, but a couple of newspaper editors in Tulsa were acutely interested.

Gordon and Mangelsdorf were covering the story of the same-sex marriages taking place in San Francisco when they reportedly decided to join in the revelry. Media reports from the time say the couple did not consult with editors at the paper before marrying.

When editors learned about what the women had done, news reports indicate, the two were removed from covering the story – likely one of the biggest of their journalism careers.

They weren't fired; they were just put on different assignments.

Although some journalists argued and still would contend that members of the media are entitled to have a personal life, Mary and I understood the paper's perspective.

In the media, it's not only the actual conflict of interest you have to worry about; it's also the appearance of conflict of interest. And Gordon and Mangelsdorf's nuptials failed on both levels, we thought. How could they cover that story while at the same time inserting themselves into the very heart of it? We didn't see how.

Although we hadn't considered whether our potential marriage in another state would have any impact on our roles as journalists in Oklahoma, we were very much aware that filing a lawsuit like we were working toward would.

The professional outcome for Gordon and Mangelsdorf resolved any lingering questions we might have had about the proper way to proceed: We knew we needed to talk to the editors in charge at the Tulsa World before the lawsuit was filed.

Coincidentally, Mary was in a meeting of upper-level editors one day discussing a wrongful-termination lawsuit that a former co-worker had filed against the newspaper.

When the meeting wrapped up, Mary was alone with then-Executive Editor Joe Worley in his office, and she broached the subject: How would the Tulsa World feel about two of its editors suing the state and federal governments for the right to marry?

Joe's reply, essentially, was that the paper probably wouldn't love it but also probably wouldn't fire us. He added that more conversations would be needed.

Shortly thereafter, Mary and I met again in Joe's office with him and then-Managing Editor Susan Ellerbach, as well as then-City Editor Wayne Greene. We laid out what we wanted to do, and we acknowledged that our actions could cause some "heartburn" for the paper.

Probably the biggest, most-public way that heartburn would be manifested was in a simple, one-sentence paragraph that, for the sake of transparency, would have to be inserted into every single story about our lawsuit for as long as it lasted – and no one had any idea then that it would last nearly a decade – that said: Bishop and Baldwin are editors at the Tulsa World.

That admission seems harmless enough, but to a cadre of readers who spend much of their time looking for evidence of a newspaper's bias, it could be a match tossed into a puddle of lighter fluid.

Never mind that when we looked around the newsroom, we saw yellow-dog liberals and deep-red conservatives alike, all working side by side, all of them journalists who left their personal politics at home and did their jobs without regard to political party or belief.

Although we were never told specifically how the Lorton family – the newspaper's owners and publishers at the time – felt about same-sex marriage, we were again assured that we wouldn't be fired for filing the lawsuit.

It was understood that we were acting as individuals, not as representatives of the paper, and there was compassion for why we felt we had to act.

Still, there would be some stipulations, as we had expected. Neither Mary nor I would have anything to do with any story about our lawsuit. This meant that our co-workers on occasion would have to edit stories that would have been our responsibility to oversee had we not been the subjects of those stories.

Although we fully understood and agreed with the condition, it was hard for us to put our co-workers in that position. This was our fight, and we hated to have to ask other people to carry any of the burden, but it would simply have to be.

With the paper's blessing, we breathed a huge sigh of relief and finally allowed ourselves to feel fully invested in the lawsuit. By this time, we knew who the plaintiffs would be, who the lawyers would be – at least initially – and who the defendants would be – at least initially.

We were on track. But trouble was coming.

CHAPTER FIVE:
THE REFERENDUM

In the same way we were paying attention to events taking place across the country with regard to same-sex marriage, so too, were the opponents of marriage equality.

Chief among them were many of the elected officials in the Oklahoma Legislature. Then-state Sen. James Williamson of Tulsa, a staunch Republican with a strong evangelical bent, proposed a referendum during the spring 2004 legislative session that would ask voters that coming November to write a ban on same-sex marriage – already codified in state statute – into the Oklahoma Constitution.

Similar moves were under way in the legislatures of at least 10 other states, but perhaps in one or two of those other states, actual doubt might have existed as to whether the measure could pass.

Such was not the case in Oklahoma. Essentially, from the moment the proposal was announced, we knew the score.

Still, the ACLU of Oklahoma tried to prevent

State Question 711 from going to the voters, filing a lawsuit on behalf of 12 couples alleging that the measure was unconstitutional because it was vague.

The opponents argued that SQ 711's language could be interpreted as to prevent common-law marriages and even subsequent marriages, such as routinely occur after a death or divorce. Dealing with more than one subject in that manner, a process called "logrolling," is illegal in Oklahoma.

The text of the amendment stated:

(a) Marriage in this state shall consist only of the union of one man and one woman. Neither this Constitution nor any other provision of law shall be construed to require that marital status or the legal incidents thereof be conferred upon unmarried couples or groups.

(b) A marriage between persons of the same gender performed in another state shall not be recognized as valid and binding in this state as of the date of the marriage.

(c) Any person knowingly issuing a marriage license in violation of this section shall be guilty of a misdemeanor.

Lawmakers, who denied the logrolling claim, and the ACLU battled back and forth for the better part of the year over the interpretation.

But neither in court papers nor in the media did the arguments ever address the merits of the central issue – whether a prohibition against marriage for same-sex couples that already existed in state statute, or the proposed ban to be added to the Oklahoma

Constitution, amounted to discrimination in violation of the U.S. Constitution.

The Oklahoma Supreme Court declined to hear the case in September 2004.

One justice complained that the protest was filed "well beyond the time when the court could consider the issue in the ordinary course of business," noting that ballots were already being printed.

Another wrote that none of the petitioners' multiple arguments identified "a single fatal state or federal constitutional flaw that facially taints the measure and would prevent it from becoming law upon the electorate's approval," adding that "the process clearly lies beyond the reach of judicial scrutiny. Unenacted measures are not law."

Of course we had hoped that the ACLU would prevail in its fight against SQ 711, but frankly, we were so disappointed at the lack of any debate over the merits of the issue – the idea that same-sex marriage was so obviously not even a plausible consideration – that we had a hard time putting any of our energy into helping the case.

Similarly, the court's ruling on technicalities left us frustrated.

Both before and after that ruling, the summer of 2004 felt like a weather metaphor brought to life.

Summers in Oklahoma can be parched and scorched, so hot and dry that we start dreaming about the smell of rain and the sweet relief it brings. Days can also be so sticky and humid that the air itself feels literally overburdened with tension, air that contains too little oxygen to get a good, deep breath out of it.

We Oklahomans know what that means. Any second, the sky will turn greenish-gray, the clouds will roll in, and the thunder and lightning will put on a show that dazzles us as much as it strikes fear in our hearts.

That summer, it was like that nearly every day, at least for the four of us as-yet-unknown plaintiffs. The vitriol that spewed forth from legislators, ministers, mayors and the proverbial man on the street made our chests tight and often hurt our hearts. And as we counted down the stifling days leading up to the election, we braced ourselves for the periodic storms.

Sen. Williamson, the Senate minority floor leader who was the chief legislative architect of the proposal, was among the speakers at a "Pro-Marriage Rally" held Aug. 24 at the Union High School Performing Arts Center in Tulsa. It had been organized by more than 40 Tulsa-area churches.

"As Christians, we are called to love homosexuals," Williamson said. "But I hope everyone at this rally knows the Scriptures prohibit homosexual acts."

The crowd of more than 4,000 people gave Williamson sustained applause when he noted that State Question 711 would also prohibit the recognition of same-sex marriages that had been legitimized by other states.

Tulsa's then-Mayor and now-Tulsa County District Judge Bill LaFortune weighed in, too, even though the proposal didn't involve municipalities in any way.

"If you believe in Christ, if you believe in this country, and if you believe in this city, you believe that marriage is a covenant between God, a man and a woman," the mayor proclaimed at the rally.

And during a videotaped message, James Dobson, the founder of the national advocacy group Focus on the Family, urged attendees to fight any attempt to extend to gay people the right to marry, warning melodramatically, "We're engaged in a critical battle, and the fate of Western civilization hangs in the balance."

The hyperbole and the hate were difficult to stomach. But the hardest part of that suffocating summer was the waiting.

As soon as we knew that the proposal was going to be on the ballot Nov. 2, we talked with our lawyers and told them to get the lawsuit ready to file the day after the election. We were going to take the war to those who would further attempt to keep us as second-class citizens. But until then, we wanted to keep quiet.

And if you know any of the four of us very well at all, you know all you need to know about why that summer was so unbearable.

But then, before we knew it, it was Election Day.

It was tough to be in the newsroom that night. As liberals living in a state that has gone from historically being among the most Democratic to today being the reddest of the red, Mary and I often had been frustrated by election results, but as journalists, the job always took precedence.

Election nights in a newsroom are crazy, even when compared with other "big news" days, but it had never been that difficult for us simply to focus on the work. We would go home afterward and pore over the election results and commiserate.

That night was different, though. As we watched the numbers pouring in, showing that ultimately 76 percent of registered Oklahoma voters who went to the polls that day voted in favor of writing discrimination into the state Constitution, we were filled with a mixture of feelings – mostly disgust and defiance.

Same-sex marriage opponents had outspent those against SQ 711 by nearly 2-to-1, but we still were heartbroken and appalled that the vote hadn't even been close.

Even in Tulsa and Oklahoma counties, the most urban, progressive areas of the state, the measure passed by more than 70 percent of the vote; in Payne and Cleveland counties, "college town" counties that often are home to liberal-leaning voters, the proposal had passed by about 68 percent.

But as angry as we were, we knew that the cannonball we had been crafting was ready to fire the following day – the proverbial shot across the bow to say that we weren't done.

We awoke on the day our lives were about to change just like we did every other day. We had breakfast, got ready for work, and drove to the office. We didn't have a press conference to announce the lawsuit's filing because it simply never occurred to us that we should.

In hindsight, I wish we had. That might have gotten more attention from our detractors and the media, all of whom likely assumed that we were ill-prepared for such a fight and treated us as such, at least in the early years.

The editors at the World knew that the filing was coming – because we had told them it was – and one of our colleagues, reporter Curtis Killman, asked us if he could interview us. We agreed and followed him to the newsroom's reception area, where he asked us a couple of questions, and then we went back to work.

That was it; it was all very low-key, very ho-hum. We didn't even stop to think about whether such an occasion should have been a bigger deal. The biggest hoopla, in fact, came from our co-workers.

About 5:30 that afternoon, Mary and I sent out across the newsroom an email in which we wrote:

"Friends and colleagues,

"By now you might know that we have filed a lawsuit challenging Oklahoma's laws and new constitutional amendment banning same-sex marriage as well as the federal Defense of Marriage Act.

"As you can imagine, it is difficult to take such an action as this as a journalist. Our profession suggests that we should not be a part of making the news, only helping to report the news. But as you also probably can imagine, this issue is terribly important to us.

"In the early stages of our discussions about this lawsuit, we asked ourselves many times, 'Why not let someone else do it?' What we kept coming back to, however, was 'If someone else, who?' 'And when?' And, finally, 'Why *not* us?'

"So we're doing it. We realize that this will affect all of you. Other City Desk editors will have to handle front-line editing of the stories about our lawsuit, and on the Copy Desk, other slots will have to handle the stories, because we will have nothing to do with them. The Tulsa World is going to have to report in stories about our lawsuit that we are, in fact, editors at the World. Your friends, relatives and even sources may give you a hard time because of our choice. But in the same sense that the Tulsa World has not tried to prevent us from taking this action, understanding that we are acting as private individuals and not as representatives of the Tulsa World, you should not be held accountable for our actions. We apologize in advance if you encounter problems. Again, we wouldn't be taking this action if it were not so vitally important to us.

"If you have any questions about how this conflict of interest will be handled at work, please feel free to ask us, (City Editor) Wayne Greene, (Executive Editor) Joe Worley or (Managing Editor) Susan Ellerbach.

"Thanks for your understanding.

"Sharon and Mary"

The response was swift and gratifying. Our co-workers replied by the dozens to wish us well and to tell us that they had our backs.

In a newsroom that fairly accurately reflected its readership, not everyone was on board, obviously. But any objectors apparently were too polite to be vocal about it, at least to us. In the nearly 10 years that passed between the lawsuit's filing and our legal marriage, that never changed.

You might think that first positive encounter would have had us feeling optimistic heading into the next day, the day when the story spread like wild-fire, not only across Oklahoma but across the entire country and beyond, but we'd be lying if we said we didn't have a case of nerves.

Still reeling from the election results just 36 hours earlier, we awoke that Thursday wondering whether some idiot would firebomb our house, whether there would be protesters in our yard, or just what was in store.

The phone began ringing early. But being second-shift workers, we got up each day about noon, so we let those calls go straight to the answering machine.

When we got out of bed and listened to the messages, we were astonished.

The first was from Betty Marriott, my first-grade teacher at Mark Twain Elementary School in Tulsa, who said, "I'm really proud of you girls." Steve Brown, who had been in the choir with Mary at the First Christian Church in Ada and also was on the faculty with her when they taught at East Central University more than a decade before, called "to make sure you're doing all right" after seeing her name in the news.

But most of the callers were strangers. One said: "You guys don't know me. I live in New York. My name is Jeff. I am sooo proud of you guys." Someone named Paul from Midwest City said he "wanted to make sure you had a friendly voice on your answering machine when you got home from work tonight" and added, "What you're doing is right and good."

At least three other callers from Oklahoma wished us well, with one saying: "I wanted to wish you the best in your efforts. Oklahoma is a very difficult place."

The friendly calls were separated only by those from reporters, including CBS News and NPR's "All Things Considered."

We kept waiting for the other shoe to drop, but it didn't. There were no protesters, no firebombs, no threatening phone calls. Sure, readers posted outrageous and disgusting comments on the online version of the Tulsa World story, but we were able to avoid those if we wanted to.

The story itself appropriately covered both sides of the issue and quoted Sen. Williamson as saying: "The radical homosexual groups have mounted court challenges to these types of laws all over the nation. ... This is their usual strategy to try to overturn the will of the people by court fiat. The only thing I'm a little bit surprised at is they are including the Defense of Marriage Act."

Williamson said he was confident that the constitutional amendment would have survived any challenges filed in state court, but he added: "It's always a question when you are dealing with the federal courts. This challenge has a possibility of going to the United States Supreme Court because that would be the ultimate decider over this issue."

Finally, we agreed with him about something.

CHAPTER SIX:
SHARON'S STORY

In the musical "Oklahoma!" the characters Curly and Jud are vying for the affection of the same woman, Laurey. In one scene, Curly asks Jud, "How'd you git to be the way you air?"

Many times over the years since we filed our lawsuit, Mary and I have been asked a version of that question, either by reporters or by someone who has heard us speak somewhere.

It's never been put forth in quite the same disgusted tone with which Curly challenges Jud, I'm pleased to say. While Jud never answers the question, Mary and I have often tried to do so.

It would be dramatic to say I popped out of the womb with a rainbow flag in one hand and a picket sign in the other. It would be poetic to say I was raised by a mother and father who protested war and the wearing of fur. But neither of those is accurate.

The truth is that a lifetime punctuated by a few painful incidents of bigotry balanced by a few shining examples of fighting back has taught me that if I was unhappy about something, the situation was mine to change.

Like most LGBT people of my generation, I knew I was different early on, even if it would be 15 to 20 years or more before I figured it out fully.

But also like most LGBT people of my generation, the "awakening" was a process, and the emotion I experienced when I first started to have an inkling of my sexual orientation wasn't some sort of relief brought on by self-realization. It was panic.

As a freshman at Central High School, thanks to being in the marching band, I quickly had a number of friends in other grades. One of my best friends, in fact, was a senior. It was a great friendship. We had similar interests, we had a lot of fun together, and we even got along well with each other's parents.

And there never was anything more to it than that. I felt no attraction to her whatsoever.

But I also felt no attraction whatsoever to a boy who fancied himself a real Romeo, an older student who seemed to see it as his goal to "conquer" as many girls as he could.

Apparently, my friend had been similarly unimpressed the previous year. So if Girl A isn't interested, and Girl B isn't interested, and Girl A and Girl B are close friends, well, clearly they are both lesbians.

At least that's how things seemed to add up for Romeo, based on the rumors he started spreading. I was mortified. My friend was surprisingly nonplussed, but then, she had the luxury of being confidently heterosexual. I was not so lucky.

Like most teenagers in a similar situation, I told no adults about what was going on, instead suffering in silence and wondering what I had done to cause this.

I was certain that anyone I told – meaning likely a straight person – would not have understood and also would have blamed me.

Although the rumors dried up over time and the incident blew over, for me, it left a mark. Whatever tiny seed of a coming-out process might have been taking root in my soul withered and died then and there.

Looking back now, of course, I have all the answers to that. I think I should call up Romeo someday and yell, "And so what if I am?!"

And it's experiences like this one that help me say to young people today, "I know what you're going through."

The specifics are different, but I know about that pit in the bottom of your stomach; the way your blood freezes in your veins; how it feels to cry yourself to sleep while thinking thoughts you don't dare tell anyone else about.

About nine years later, while a student at the University of Oklahoma in Norman, I began to come to terms with whom, by then, I knew I was.

Coming out while away at college offered me some security that a lot of LGBT people don't have, especially minors still dependent on their parents, and I was a little older – 23. But I don't think that tiny bit of added age necessarily translated into a better handling of what is easily one of the toughest transitions in any person's life.

I began going to the weekly meetings of OU's Gay, Lesbian, Bisexual Alliance. I don't remember a thing about the content of the first meeting I attended because I spent the entire time looking around at everyone there and thinking: "Really? All these people are gay?" Like most LGBT people, I had been pretty certain, at least for a short time, that I was the only homosexual person in the world.

But within a few weeks, I was beginning to feel like I belonged not only to the GLBA but also to this larger group, and I was beginning to believe the other students and our occasional speakers when they said we were normal and fine.

After our meeting one week, some of the women decided to go to the Lower Deck, a bar just off campus that was having "ladies night."

But just as a few of us stragglers arrived, others of our group were leaving, apparently amid some controversy. It seems that some of the women in our group had gotten up to slow dance, and the bar's owner — saying other patrons were complaining — asked them to leave.

They said she told them, "You're not the kind of ladies we're looking for." Some of our women later said the bartender had written "No dykes" on a blackboard above the bar, as well. After some disagreement and protest, our group left.

Reading news reports from the time, I'm struck today by two things. The first is how common the

ignorance and bigotry were. This is from The Oklahoman, the state's largest newspaper:

"Some (lesbians) showed up and they started
growing in numbers. It made some customers uncomfortable. She (the bar owner) said she identified
'lesbians' as those with certain styles of 'haircuts, T-
shirts and AIDS awareness buttons and ribbons.'
She alleges that 'lesbians' 'screamed about women's
rights' while in the club."

And then there was this:

"Asked if she felt the word 'dyke' is derogatory,
she (the bar owner) said no. 'Black is black, white is
white and dyke is dyke.' "

The second thing that struck me is how much I
don't remember from nearly 25 years ago!

For example, the stories from The Oklahoman
say the bar "was the location of sit-ins, demonstra-
tions and protests." I remember only one demonstration. Did I go to only one? I can't say.

What I *do* know is that the demonstration in
which I participated is one of those foundational
blocks I was standing on when Gay and Sue and
Mary and I filed our lawsuit more than a decade later.

Sure, I was angry that this group of my friends
was being mistreated. Sure, I thought the bar owner's actions were illegal, or at least should have been.
But I don't think it was until that one evening that I
understood discrimination as a victim of it.

We marched in a circle with Oklahoma City-area
singer-songwriter and social-justice activist Peggy

Johnson leading us in singing "We Shall Overcome" and "Singing for Our Lives" ("We Are a Gentle, Angry People").

In that moment, I understood bigger words than anger. I understood indignation. I understood determination. I understood solidarity in the way that even though I knew only a few of the people marching with me, we were clearly sisters and brothers.

I understood a somberness or sadness that comes with the realization that this thing – in my case this fight for equality – would be with me for the rest of my days.

In the end, complaints were filed with the city of Norman's Human Rights Commission, but the commission dismissed them because "matters of sexual preference" were not covered under the city ordinance on discrimination.

That has changed in 25 years.

Norman's City Council voted unanimously in December 2015 in favor of a resolution acknowledging inclusive protections for lesbian, gay, bisexual and transgender residents. The resolution – albeit a non-binding one – was drafted by the city's Human Rights Commission.

Some of the details from that time may be fuzzy today, but the lesson is still crystal clear: Stand up for yourself. Do what's right. Never give up.

The women who helped fight that fight – Peggy Johnson, Pat Reaves, Helen and Tina Stiefmiller, Margaret Cox and many others – taught me that.

Hollywood likes a story with drama, and I can only imagine what a filmmaker might do with a story like "The Lower Deck Dust-up."

But our lives aren't made up of Hollywood drama for the most part. Our lives are made up of small moments – often seemingly insignificant at the time – involving people who one day we will realize were helping us to become the people we are.

Sometimes those people play a fleeting role in your life, coming into it briefly, serving a purpose, and then moving on. At other times, the people who help shape you, well, that's what they were put here to do.

My parents' 10-acre property west of downtown Tulsa backs up to the Arkansas River. In fact, the property deed goes to the middle of the river channel, but the county oversees a flood-control levee that stretches across the back part of the property.

It's not uncommon to see a county vehicle driving down the levee, but this has never been a problem; any problems have been a result of outsiders who occasionally saw our property as public access to the river. Dad was always quick to let them know they were mistaken, and that was usually the end of it.

But during the late 1970s, someone proposed creating a running path along the top of the levee. That might sound like a neat idea – unless you're the homeowner whose property would be transgressed by hundreds of strangers each day.

Dad and Mom and some neighbors formed a group – Citizens Against the Running Path – and successfully fought the plan.

It's not like they took their cause to the Supreme Court, I realize. But while other kids' parents might have been talking about being pushed around by "the man" and teaching their children that you can't fight city hall, my parents showed me that you can.

In a thousand other ways – many very small and a few very large – Richard and Helen Baldwin also taught me those foundational lessons: Stand up for yourself. Do what's right. Never give up.

By the time we were thinking about a marriage-equality lawsuit in 2004 and were asking ourselves all those questions about whether someone else could or would take on the fight, and if so, who, and when, we couldn't have been better prepared to know the answer in our hearts: Stand up for yourself. Do what's right. Never give up.

CHAPTER SEVEN:
MARY'S STORY

Mary and I have been together for 20 years, but that means she lived 35 years before I came into her life. Obviously, her answer to the question, "How'd you get to be the way you are?" is different from mine. I'll let her tell it in her own words:

———

I've always been one to think for myself, rarely going along with the crowd just to please others. I think I was born with an independent streak and then developed a headstrong attitude to go along with it.

Yet I led a sheltered life as a child and teenager. I really knew nothing of worldly ways or the world much beyond small-town Ada, Oklahoma, so because I had never been exposed to people who were openly gay, I had no real idea that being gay was even within the realm of possibility for me or anyone else I knew.

Until I fell in love for the first time, that is. And then I knew: This isn't wrong. People say it's wrong, but I know what I feel, and I know right from wrong, and this is not wrong; this is so *very* right.

To shine a light on what makes me me, let's back up a bit, all the way back to the fourth grade. I attended McLish School from the middle of the third grade through high school graduation.

McLish was a small public school out in the country near Fittstown, a town of a few hundred people about 10 miles south of Ada, population around 15,000.

We still lived in Ada when my mother accepted a job teaching at McLish Grade School when I was in the third grade, and my brother and I transferred from our elementary school in Ada to McLish at that time. The school was so small that sometimes two grades shared a classroom.

When I was in the fourth grade, my homeroom teacher – who was prominent in the First Baptist Church of Ada – told our class that the peace symbol was a broken, upside-down cross and that no Christian should ever wear one.

My classmates all turned to look at me, knowing that I frequently wore a leather ponytail holder with a metal peace symbol on it. I was incensed that our teacher had said that and that now, having "learned my lesson," I would be expected to no longer wear that simple hair accessory.

But the lesson I learned was that the teacher is not always right. When some of my classmates saw me wearing the hair accessory on a subsequent day, they said, "Ummmm! Mary's wearing that broken cross!"

I told them that some people might think it was what our teacher had proclaimed it to be, but I didn't. To me – and to many people – it was a symbol of peace, and I would continue to wear it.

The First Baptist Church of Ada was the largest church in town when I was growing up in the 1960s and '70s. I was raised in the First Christian Church (Disciples of Christ), which was catty-corner across Broadway from the First United Methodist Church, and the First Baptist Church, a Southern Baptist congregation, was another block south on Broadway. Many of the city's most prominent business people and educators – including my fourth-grade teacher – were members of that church.

It seemed to me that their faith was in words and that they thought if I didn't use the same theological lingo they did, I wasn't a Christian.

When I was in the early years of grade school, the neighbor children I played with would ask me: "Are you saved?" and I would respond: "What do you mean 'saved'? We don't use that term in our church, but I am a Christian. Is that what you mean?" But they continued to insist that I had to be "saved" – and to use that word.

My father, Thurston Bishop, was employed by a member of the First Baptist Church, and when I was young, he often invited my father to bring the family to one of his church's revivals.

We went sometimes, and we'd sit there night after

night listening to the preacher tell people to hold up their hands if they loved the Lord and wanted Jesus to come into their lives, and then there was always the altar call: "Come down to the front if you want Jesus to come into your life, and we'll pray over you."

What was a child to think? "Does this church know something my church doesn't? Why don't we do that? Am I supposed to get up and go down to the front? Why are my parents not going down to the front? If I don't go, people will think I don't love Jesus! But I do, and that's between him and me! Who are they to tell me what to do to prove that I love Jesus? I'm not like them. I don't have to be told what to do, and I don't have to do what they say."

It just made me so mad – and uncomfortable.

In high school, the youth group at my church was small but sincere. Those of us who were the core group truly wanted to be the best disciples we could be, "living for Jesus a life that is true, striving to please him in all that I do." The youth group at the First Baptist Church, on the other hand, was massive, with hundreds of teenagers showing up for parties after Friday night Ada High School home football games.

My best friend, who was from my church but went to Ada High, and I went to one of those Friday night youth events once, just to see for ourselves what it was like and why that church could attract so many young people while ours couldn't.

What we saw was a mass of young people all focused on being in the cool group, being seen with the popular people. It was a dimly-lit party, complete with free food, drinks and music. As we saw it, that's what the kids were flocking there for, and it made me sick.

While the Baptist kids were all at the huge Falls Creek church camp in the summers, those of us from First Christian met with others from Disciples of Christ congregations across southern Oklahoma at Texoma Christian Camp. Our camps usually had about 40 campers and a handful of counselors, and some of us became very close friends.

I remember attending a small group session on "Homosexuality and Christianity" at camp when I was in high school in the late '70s.

A minister who was a camp counselor led the session, which was held in one of the cabins. Before the session started, several of the girls acted like they were making out with each other on the beds – their way of making fun of "homosexuals." I thought to myself: "They are making fun of people they don't even know who didn't choose to be gay but were made that way by God."

I had no inkling at that point that I was gay, but I knew that the girls' behavior was hurtful and wrong. The counselor talked to us about what homosexuality was and said there were different theories on whether it was a chosen or inherent orientation, and he said religious people also had different thoughts on the subject of nurture vs. nature.

He let us know that not everyone in society or

even in the church thought homosexuality was a sin.

My family was not among those who didn't think it was a sin.

I remember watching the television news with my mother one evening when I was a teenager and seeing a story about a group of gay people having a sit-in at the Oklahoma Capitol. At least that's how I remember it. I can't figure out now what that sit-in was about or what gay Oklahomans were brave enough to participate in the 1970s.

But I will never forget my mother saying, "Isn't that disgusting?" I thought to myself: "No. It's not disgusting. Why would it be disgusting? They're just people."

Then, when I found myself falling in love with another woman during my second semester of college, my mother saw it before I really knew what was happening. Just 18, I still lived at home and attended East Central University. I was extremely naïve, and when I realized the attraction I had for this girl, I was scared. Did this mean I was a homosexual, one of those people society considers "disgusting," "vile" and "deviant" and who are said to be "an abomination to God"?

But I knew that what I felt for her was right. I knew that I would know if it were wrong. My conscience was clear, but I was still very scared. I didn't know any gay people – or at least I didn't know that I knew any gay people – so there must not be any others around here, and maybe *she* wasn't gay but it was just me.

Finally one night, I got up the nerve to ask her to kiss me. She refused at first, because she, too, was afraid. But I was persistent, and eventually she did kiss me. I had never felt such bliss, and I knew it was right.

It's just that the rest of the world didn't know it was right, and we could be kicked out of our parents' homes and expelled from school, and we could lose our jobs and be kicked out of our churches over this. We had to keep it a secret.

Yet while I knew that being gay was not a sin, I believed that lying about it would be. Therefore, when my mother finally asked me one evening if this new friend was a lesbian, I answered, "Well, if she is, she's not the only one."

Thus began my coming out – and my moving out.

My family did not take the revelation well. I never wanted to hurt my parents, so I tried to do what they told me was right, and I told the love of my young life that I couldn't see her any more. But I was miserable, and I cried constantly for a week.

Eventually I realized that I couldn't live my life for other people – that I had to do what *I* knew to be right, no matter what.

And so a week later I started seeing her again, and when my father found out, he gave me a 5:30 p.m. curfew so I wouldn't have time to see her after school and work. And that did it. I had never had a curfew in my life! I had always been a "good girl," and now, at age 18, I had a 5:30 curfew?

I told my parents that I was an adult and that I

was moving out. My girlfriend was 19 and also lived with her parents. My parents called her parents to tell them about the nature of our relationship, and she moved out, too. We rented an apartment together, and within three days of the imposition of that 5:30 curfew, I was gone.

I was thrilled to be with my girlfriend on our own, but I was still afraid. I felt like I had a scarlet "L" on my forehead and that everywhere I went, everyone would know that I was a lesbian.

In those days, people felt free to tell gay jokes, and a student in several of my college classes made it clear that he hated gay people, frequently saying things such as "they ought to round up all the queers and kill them or at least put them on an island somewhere."

And everyone, including me, had to listen to his bigotry. Even the teacher said nothing to stop him. It was just OK in those days to hate gay people. Bigotry against gays was accepted as normal then; being gay was not.

So I sat there in silence, wanting to say: "Is that how you feel about me? You say you're my friend, but I'm gay. Do you want to kill me?" But I didn't. I couldn't. I had too much fear.

Not knowing that I knew any other gay people when I found myself falling in love for the first time, I was a mess. Fortunately, my part-time job was working as a secretary for a community mental health center. Even though it was part time, it came with benefits, including insurance and paid vacation.

While all that was great, the best benefit for me was getting to know one of the clinicians at the time, Cassia Mealor, and Pat Reaves, who had been a counseling intern there. And yes, this was the same Pat Reaves who later was a mentor to Sharon at OU. This is just one of many examples of how Sharon's and my lives have intersected in some odd ways.

Pat and Cassia lived together, and I saw several similarities between their relationship and my relationship with my girlfriend. Could they also be lesbians?

I wanted – no, needed – so badly to know, but I couldn't just ask them. If they weren't, they would be insulted! And besides, there just *weren't* other gay people in Ada. There couldn't be. It was just me. And her.

But I was an emotional wreck, so finally one day I went upstairs to Cassia's office and asked if I could talk to her. I closed the door and sat down in the "client's" recliner. And I continued to sit there. She gently asked me what I wanted to tell her, but I just couldn't get the words to come out of my mouth.

Although *I* didn't think there was anything wrong with being gay, I thought everyone else did, so I knew I would be risking everything if I said it out loud. But I needed emotional help, so after an excruciatingly long period of silence, I finally told her that my friend and I were "more than just friends."

Cassia later told me that she and Pat had also seen the similarities in our relationships and had been afraid that my friend was a lesbian who had fallen for me but that I wasn't and would be crushed when I learned that she was in love with me.

So when I came out to her in her office that day, she breathed a sigh of relief and told me it was going to be all right. She and Pat took us under their wings and were the mentors all gay kids need.

They taught us that there was a whole community of gay men and lesbians out there – including right there in Ada in 1980 – and they introduced us to new friends and a new way of thinking.

They introduced me to women's music and feminism and working for women's rights. And they are the ones who helped me move my personal belongings out of my parents' house when the time came to do that.

I owe so much of my development into adulthood, into being a feminist and an activist – my truly finding myself – to them. I truly believe that had it not been for Pat and Cassia, I would have killed myself during those early, very scary days of realizing that I am gay.

But they were my rock, and I've always wanted to be for young LGBT people what they were for me.

After college, I worked for a year and then went to grad school. Then I was a reporter for a twice-weekly newspaper in Bristow, a small town in Oklahoma where I came out in a newspaper column as a feminist but not as a lesbian.

Then I went to work for The Daily Oklahoman, which surely was one of the most conservative newspapers in the country, so even though I had a girlfriend in Oklahoma City at the time, I was not out at work.

Then, in 1986, I returned to Ada to teach journalism at my alma mater, East Central University. Of course, I couldn't be openly gay there, either, because I still could have been fired for violating the "moral turpitude" clause in all faculty members' contracts.

But I had a long-term girlfriend, and we lived together in Ada, and I would take her to departmental functions as if we were a couple. I just wasn't *saying* we were a couple. It surely was one of those things where most everyone knew but no one was saying anything publicly.

The same was true at church. I was in the choir and was on the diaconate at the First Christian Church and was the secretary of the board, and around 1994 I was serving on a pastoral search committee that had narrowed the field of candidates down to two.

We were leaning toward one, but he informed our chairwoman before he came for a visit that his daughter was a lesbian and that he accepted her fully – and he wanted any church that called him as its minister to know that up front.

Well, that turned the tide for the committee, and just before a vote was to be taken to issue a call to the other candidate, I found a shred of courage and came out publicly.

I sat in that meeting in the Fellowship Hall and told those committee members that by saying that man wasn't worthy of being our minister, they were saying my deceased father hadn't been worthy of being an elder in our church, that my mother shouldn't have taught Sunday school, that I wasn't worthy of being in the choir or serving as a deacon or being on the church board or being on that very committee.

My heart pounded and my voice shook throughout the impromptu speech, but no one else made a sound until well after I was through.

Then they hugged me and told me they loved me but that this wasn't about me – that they were afraid this issue would tear the church apart if we called that minister.

I told them that I thought this man was exactly what our church needed because I certainly was not the only gay person to have come out of that church – that I could think of five church families off the top of my head who had gay children and had never been able to talk about it.

I told them that these members *needed* to have a minister who would talk about it and tell them that it's OK, that God loves their children, too. But I said that if they still felt that way, I would go along with them in voting to call the other minister because we needed unanimity and I didn't want to be the lone holdout.

I have always regretted that vote. I had found the courage to tell the people on that committee – people who were my friends – how they had hurt me, but I didn't have enough courage to vote no when they were all voting yes.

In those days in small-town Oklahoma, gay people could be semi-closeted and semi-out. A person could *be* gay and get along in society as long as he or she didn't "make an issue of it." It was as if the military's new-at-the-time "Don't Ask, Don't Tell" policy extended to all of society. You could be a respectable member of the community and keep your job as long as you didn't talk about being gay. And it wasn't polite for others to ask if you were gay. It just couldn't be talked about.

So when Vice President Al Gore spoke in Tulsa in 1993, several of us wannabe activists from around the state converged outside Tulsa's convention center to protest the new policy.

It was a silent protest, and we put masking tape across our mouths and wrote the words "Don't Ask" or "Don't Tell" on the tape. We also carried signs on poster board.

When a couple of TV stations' reporters came over, cameras in tow, to interview us about why we were there, those of us who couldn't afford to be seen on TV covered our faces with our signs. If my face had been seen at a protest of an anti-gay policy, I most assuredly would have lost my job the very next day.

During my last year at East Central, I butted heads with the administration over freedom of the student press and academic freedom issues, and I lost my job over that.

While the battle was raging, my department chairman told me that I needed to "choose my battles." That was good advice. I don't think he expected that I would follow through with that particular battle, but I did.

I went into it knowing that I didn't have the safety net of tenure because I hadn't finished my doctorate and likely would be fired, but I maintained that my integrity was more important than any job.

That decision – and the resulting job search – led me to the Tulsa World, which hired me as an editor in 1995 after East Central "declined to renew my contract." And that led me to Sharon, the love of my life.

I've learned to take a step out in faith that as long as I'm doing what I believe to be right, things will work out for the best. That gives me courage.

Even though things we go through might be scary, they are stepping stones to where we need to be. I wouldn't trade the hard times I've had, because they've brought me to where I am today, making me stronger along the way.

Sharon and I always say that "the journey *is* the destination," and we intend to savor every mile of the trip.

We also are very aware that times are changing such that being out is much easier today than when I was coming out to myself in 1980 and even than when we filed our lawsuit in 2004.

It's easier because of all of those who came before us, pushing their own closet doors a little bit at a time or busting them wide open.

We could not be where we are today without

them – and without the previous journeys we've taken ourselves.

In working for equality, social justice, understanding and acceptance, we always build on the foundations laid by those who came before us, and we hold tight to the belief that over time, things will improve.

Because of that belief, my motto has long been the chorus of "The Rock Will Wear Away," a song by women's music pioneers Holly Near and Meg Christian. It serves as a kind of rallying cry to continue working for change, even when it seems that we're getting nowhere:

"Can we be like drops of water falling on the stone,
splashing, breaking, dispersing in air?
Weaker than the stone by far, but be aware that
as time goes by, the rock will wear away."

CHAPTER EIGHT:
THE UNEXPECTED OPPOSITION

It didn't take many days after our lawsuit was filed for the euphoria to begin to wear off, although much to our amazement, the damper on our enthusiasm was coming from the most unlikely of places – leaders of the gay-rights movement.

As soon as word of our lawsuit began to spread across the country, we started hearing from some of the national LGBT rights groups. You might think they would be calling to congratulate us on our gutsy stand and offer support, if not financially, at least morally. But such was not the case.

These groups wanted us to drop our challenge of the federal Defense of Marriage Act. They said we were going to lose and that in doing so, we would "set the cause back 20 years."

We were stunned. We had prepared for backlash and even outrage, but not from within the LGBT community.

Mary and I and Gay and Sue met with our lawyers to discuss how to proceed, and even in the early days of the case, we were almost always on the same page or at least in the same chapter when such questions arose.

In this case, it was clear and simple – thanks for your input, but we think you're wrong, so we'll continue on as planned.

We thought that would be the end of it, but instead, representatives from some of the national LGBT rights groups then said they wanted to meet with us. We weren't inclined to agree, but at the same time, we reasoned, maybe a face-to-face meeting would give them an opportunity to make us see more clearly why they thought as they did.

The Oklahoma ACLU chapter agreed to host the meeting late on a weekday afternoon at its office in Oklahoma City.

In attendance were we four plaintiffs, our lawyers – Kay, Tim and Roy Tucker, who worked for Kay, some LGBT community leaders from the Oklahoma City area, and representatives from some of the national groups, including the Human Rights Campaign and the national office of the ACLU.

The national folks again presented their case as to why we should drop our DOMA challenge, but, in fact, there was nothing about it to see more clearly. It was the same argument we understood it to be after the initial contact – they said they thought we would lose at the Supreme Court and that an adverse ruling there would "set the cause back 20 years."

On the other hand, they were afraid we might *win*, and, to their thinking, Congress would be so outraged that it would attempt to pass the Federal Marriage Amendment – which would have written a ban on same-sex marriage into the U.S. Constitution.

We simply couldn't have disagreed more.

We wondered aloud whether perhaps they had forgotten eighth-grade civics, where we learned that even if Congress were to pass such an amendment (two-thirds of both the House and the Senate would have to be in agreement even to reach that point), a full three-quarters of the legislatures of the 50 states would then have to ratify the amendment for it to become law.

Although this path has been traveled successfully 27 times in U.S. history (but only 10 times in the last century), the process is laborious at best.

Indeed, the Equal Rights Amendment, which would have granted full equality to women, a seemingly simple and amenable concept, never achieved more than 35 of the 38 states needed for ratification. Even after Congress extended the deadline for ratification from 1979 to 1982, the proposal expired with only 30 states on board after some went back on their votes.

And these organizations wanted us to believe, at a time of ever-growing acceptance of LGBT people and issues, and when same-sex couples were already marrying in Massachusetts without the world collapsing, that both houses of Congress and the legislatures of 38 states would ratify an amendment to the U.S. Constitution to keep same-sex couples from marrying?

We thought that was preposterous. We still do.

So the national groups' representatives went their way and we went ours, but the hard feelings lingered. We had never asked for or expected a dime of financial support from these national LGBT rights groups, but we were deeply disappointed that they wouldn't even cheer us on.

I have come to believe that as much as anything, their problem with us was that we just weren't doing things *their* way. They had a plan. They ostensibly were going to fight for same-sex marriage rights in the "easy" states without challenging DOMA, and after they had enough state victories racked up, they would make a national push for marriage equality "when the time was right."

The problem with that, for us, is that we don't live in the low-hanging fruit states of New England or the West Coast. Oklahoma was never a part of their plan. Oklahoma was always a flyover state that they assumed would get swept along and swept up in their grand victory.

But that wasn't good enough for us. Why, we asked, should we sit back and wait for our rights to be handed to us in due course? That's not who we are. That's not who we *ever* were.

My cover photo on my Facebook page is frequently a picture of a huge granite bench that sits in the Georgia Aquarium in honor of philanthropists Billi and Bernie Marcus. Bernie Marcus, a cofounder and longtime CEO of The Home Depot, and his wife gave $250 million toward the aquarium's creation, and in exchange, they got a fabulous bench. But for me, the words engraved into the bench outweigh the granite of which it is made:

History is written
By those who make the wake
Not by those who ride on it
Nor by those who
Watch safely from the shore

I can't help but smile at the irony – that words engraved on a bench to honor a staunch conservative (who no longer has any ties to the home-improvement store chain, for the record) have, for the better part of a decade, been a rallying cry for a marriage-equality fighter in Oklahoma.

But those words are why we declined to follow the lead of the national LGBT rights groups with regard to the fight for marriage equality. We believed that LGBT Oklahomans had a right to be a part of the national conversation on marriage equality, a right to have a role in writing history.

In retrospect, we have to acknowledge that the national groups pretty much achieved their piece-meal victory plan.

Prior to June 2013, when the U.S. Supreme Court decided *United States v. Windsor*, the case that struck down Section 2 of DOMA, eight states and the District of Columbia had attained marriage equality.

By the time the high court struck down all state bans on same-sex marriage and made DOMA's Section 3 a moot point in June 2015 in *Obergefell v. Hodges*, 36 states and D.C. already had legalized marriage for same-sex couples.

Oklahoma was not among the last 14 states to be caught up in that monumental victory, however, having achieved marriage equality nearly nine months earlier, on Oct. 6, 2014. So I guess we got our way, too.

In April 2015, on the evening before the Supreme Court hearings in the *Obergefell* case, Gay, Sue, Mary and I attended a historic reception in Washington, D.C. – some 200 plaintiffs from 33 states representing more than 55 marriage-equality-related cases spanning about 40 years gathered in one place.

Also in attendance was national Freedom to Marry founder Evan Wolfson, who had also shunned our case, personally at one point. In a show of good sportsmanship of sorts, Mary told him, "We had different ideas about how to get there, but we wound up at the same place."

That might be true. But Oklahoma wasn't last. We made sure of it.

CHAPTER NINE:
THE NEW BEGINNING

No amount of being brave, no abundance of stamina can prepare a person for the nearly five-year drought of activity we experienced after filing the lawsuit in 2004.

When the initial interest died down after a few days, Mary and I went back to our regular lives, but with an eye toward being ready at any second to spring into action as court developments warranted. Instead, we waited. And we waited. And periodically, we would get a copy of a filing in the mail from the lawyer's office showing that the case did, in fact, still exist.

But what lawyers know and don't often tell clients is that lawsuits are tedious! Claims are made in a filing. Rebuttals are made in another filing. Responses to the rebuttals are made in another filing. Responses to the responses are made in another filing. And so on, *ad infinitum.*

It's easy to understand why we were frustrated. We had not expected the case to drag on to such an extent, and although we four plaintiffs were its central figures, we were also the ones least in control of its pace.

Looking back, it's astonishing how much time passed with little or no movement in the case. We would go entire weeks, sometimes two or three, even, without thinking about this "thing" we had, this thing that it seemed hardly anyone knew about, this thing that most people, frankly, probably thought was folly, if they thought about it at all.

Our only true organized support during that time came from Gay and Sue's church, Community of Hope United Church of Christ.

Its minister, the Rev. Leslie Penrose, had stepped down as a clergy member of the United Methodist Church under fire for her support of same-sex marriage several years earlier, and she and her flock had affiliated with the United Church of Christ. Not everyone at Community of Hope was LGBT, but their theology was completely accepting and affirming.

Right after the lawsuit was filed, they held a prayer service for the four of us. And although it was a relatively small church, the congregation held a benefit variety show and silent auction and gave the entire proceeds to us, the seed money for a lawsuit fund the church managed for us. Church members themselves were among the fund's most regular and generous contributors.

It felt strange to us not to be aligned with the local LGBT rights organization. But we were not affiliated with Oklahomans for Equality yet, and OkEq was led at the time by people whose beliefs were in line with those of the national groups. We were stung a little bit that they hadn't reached out to us. We couldn't understand why they didn't realize that we were fighting for them, too, or, perhaps more importantly, that Oklahoma deserved to be in the fight to begin with.

Happily, that distance didn't last too awfully long. In October 2008, the four of us plaintiffs were contacted by Toby Jenkins, who had recently become president of the board of directors of Oklahomans for Equality.

Although we weren't allied with OkEq, Mary and I had had a strange habit of running into Toby around town for years, including at a restaurant where he had worked while we were celebrating an anniversary.

We knew who he was; he knew who we were; and we all were always friendly, but we were still surprised when he invited the four of us to his apartment for brunch one weekend, along with Nancy McDonald, the founder of Tulsa's chapter of PFLAG – or Parents, Families and Friends of Lesbians and Gays.

Nancy, who had been PFLAG's national president in 1998-99, knew a bit about the fight for marriage equality. Back in May 1996, when she was PFLAG's national vice president, she had testified before the U.S. House of Representatives Judiciary Committee's Subcommittee on the Constitution regarding the Defense of Marriage Act.

U.S. Rep. Steve Largent, a Republican who represented Oklahoma's 1st District, which includes Tulsa, was a co-sponsor of DOMA in the House, and the proposal was introduced in the Senate by Sen. Don Nickles, also an Oklahoma Republican.

I note this here to show that hatred of the LGBT community by Oklahoma's elected officials is not a new phenomenon; 21 years ago, two members of our state's congressional delegation were leading the charge to strip away any civil rights LGBT people ever thought about having.

It was in that climate that Nancy sat before the committee on May 15, 1996, and told the panel about the value of her then-39-year marriage; about her divided family – how three of her four children had legally married the person they loved but that her fourth child could not; about how the Defense of Marriage Act said to her, to her straight children and to her lesbian daughter, as well as to millions of Americans, that, in fact, Americans are *not* all created equally, nor are they to be treated equally under the law.

Nancy's remarks were impassioned, but ultimately they fell on deaf ears. DOMA eventually passed the House and Senate with overwhelming, veto-proof margins and was signed into law by then-President Bill Clinton in the fall of 1996.

But the defeat hadn't ended the fight for Nancy. Here we were, more than 12 years later, sitting in Toby's living room with one of the legends of the battle, still talking about marriage equality.

Toby told us we were there that day to hear his apology for the local LGBT leaders who went before him and sided against us. They had been wrong not to support us, he said, and he was ashamed. He vowed that from that point forward, Oklahomans for Equality would have our backs, whenever and however necessary. He said a lot of making amends needed to be done.

We were surprised, pleasantly so, and relieved, as well.

Although we made it clear to Toby that legal and other decisions about the case would continue to rest solely with the four of us – a point with which he took no issue – it is true that we were weary of standing mostly alone.

Sure, we had the unflinching support of some family members and close friends, and yes, Sue and Gay's church was still behind us, but in a sense, we had no home base, no foundation, no bedrock.

Toby's apology – even on behalf of people who still didn't support us – was welcomed and appreciated. And now we would go forward a little less alone. At least we could say we had the support of the LGBT leadership in Tulsa, even if there was dissent in some quarters of the LGBT community at large about whether our lawsuit should even exist.

And the timing couldn't have been better, because court developments were threatening the future of the case itself.

Our first ruling in the case had come about two years earlier, in August 2006. In it, Judge Kern had said Mary and I didn't have "standing" to sue the federal government over the Defense of Marriage Act. Standing is a legal term that means you have sufficient evidence to try to prove that you have suffered harm as a result of something, in this case, DOMA.

But Kern said DOMA's purpose was to allow the federal government not to recognize the marriages of same-sex couples and to allow states not to recognize same-sex marriages that were legal in other jurisdictions. Mary and I had no legal marriage of any kind, and thus no marriage for any government to recognize or not, so we had no standing.

Judge Kern allowed Sue and Gay, however, to continue the DOMA challenge because their May 2005 Canadian marriage license gave them standing.

And here we were in early 2009 – yes, 2½ years after Judge Kern's ruling – and we were finally getting a ruling from the 10th Circuit on the appeals related to the 2006 ruling.

We have no idea why the case lingered for so long at the 10th Circuit U.S. Court of Appeals, and lawyers tend to be reticent to hypothesize about such things. But the appellate judges affirmed Judge Kern's ruling that Mary and I could not challenge DOMA.

We were still in the Oklahoma part of the challenge, however, and by then, Sue and Gay had also married in California, so they were left in the DOMA challenge.

Importantly, the 10th Circuit judges also ruled that we had sued the wrong defendants in the state part of the case and removed the governor and state attorney general as defendants.

The judges went a step further – they wrote that we should have sued the Tulsa County court clerk, whose office issues marriage licenses. Such direct instruction from an appellate court was seen as unusual.

But the mixed-bag ruling from the courts wasn't our only concern; some other bad news had been building for a while. Our lawyer, Kay, had been increasingly beset by some chronic health issues as well as some issues with her firm.

One solution that allowed her to keep working in some fashion was to petition the court to excuse her from all of her federal cases, including ours.

Although the court did not rule on that request for some time – again, we don't know why – the delay gave us time to start looking for a new lawyer.

With the clock ticking, Mary and I began making phone calls. But not just any attorney would do.

This lawyer needed to have the skill set to potentially take the case to the U.S. Supreme Court. This lawyer needed the autonomy to be able to do this without worrying about being fired from a firm that didn't agree with marriage equality and/or didn't want to allow one of its revenue generators to devote so much time to a pro-bono civil-rights case.

Yet this lawyer, if not independently wealthy, needed the support of a deep-pocketed firm to take on such a case.

The yellow pages weren't going to be much help.

We called several local lawyers about possibly taking the case, but those conversations were tricky.

For starters, we didn't want them to think the case was on the ropes. No one wants to be part of a losing team. Secondly, we couldn't really ask them to take the case until it was official that we needed someone to do so. Thirdly, we didn't want to formally ask them to take it until we'd decided formally if we *wanted* them to take it!

So a lot of the conversations were couched in very hypothetical terms – if the case were to be in need of a new lawyer, might you be interested in being considered, and if so, might you have the resources ... .

It was all feeling a bit cloak and dagger.

All of the local attorneys we spoke with expressed support for our intent while making it clear that they were not the superhero we sought. It was simply too much to ask. We understood, truly, but we had to press on.

Eventually, we realized that we needed to swallow our pride a bit and start looking at the national LGBT groups' legal representatives. Maybe one of them had had a change of heart over the years and would take our case.

Our first entreaty was to Cheryl Jacques, a former Massachusetts lawmaker who had been the first openly lesbian member of that state's Senate, where she served six terms.

Jacques also had been president of the Human Rights Campaign for 11 months in 2004, when the HRC was among the national groups coming out against our lawsuit, but she had left HRC late that year, citing "a difference in management philosophy" with her board following criticism of HRC's inability to defeat ballot measures in 11 states, including Oklahoma, outlawing same-sex marriage.

A quote on her website seemed telling to us: "The lessons of history are clear – Equality cannot wait for a convenient time; society only moves toward equality when challenged to do so. Change does not come through cautious inaction but through principled insistence."

Our hope was that the philosophical difference meant she supported lawsuits such as ours and would be willing to represent us. Although she was sympathetic and, indeed, seemed to support our efforts, she told us she was not in a position to take on our case.

Our second call was to Evan Wolfson, the aforementioned founder of Freedom to Marry.

Evan had never supported our case, and in truth we didn't expect him to do so then, either. But we were desperate, and we thought he might be willing to overlook our fundamental differences and at least point us in the direction of a lawyer who could meet our needs.

We were wrong. Evan said he still did not support our DOMA challenge, would not help us, and would not direct us to any other lawyers. He was curt and unhelpful, and he insincerely wished us well as he hung up the phone.

That was the last time we spoke to him until the

plaintiffs reception in Washington the night before the Supreme Court hearings in the *Obergefell* case. And by then, we were married.

But just about the time things seemed hopeless, luck shined on us. The rulings from the 10th Circuit had garnered a little bit of media attention, and one story about the case caught the eye of Don Holladay of the Holladay Chilton law firm in Oklahoma City.

Don and his wife, Kay Holladay, have a gay son among their three children, and Kay had co-founded PFLAG Norman in 1995.

Don, who was nearing retirement, saw an opportunity to do his part in righting a wrong. He called Kay Bridger-Riley and asked whether she would be interested in having some help with the Bishop case.

Kay immediately called the four of us to tell us the news, and before the week was out, Sue, Gay, Mary and I had traveled to the Holladays' Norman home to discuss the possibility of Don's taking the case.

Years later, on the first anniversary of our ruling from Judge Kern, Don – in one of his exceedingly rare "mushy moments" – called our alliance "a pact made over the living room table" that none of us realized then would turn out as it had. We thought he was the perfect lawyer. He called us his dream clients. A mutual admiration society was blossoming.

But the case … the case was in a bit of a mess after the 10th Circuit's rulings.

Don thought he saw a way forward, and we had faith in him. He brought an associate from his firm, James C. Warner III, onto the case, and they got to work. Within a week, they had created an amended complaint that bore little resemblance to the original filing.

Based on that unexpected guidance from the 10th Circuit in its recent ruling, the amended complaint added Tulsa County Court Clerk Sally Howe Smith as a defendant, dropped as defendants Oklahoma's governor and attorney general and the president of the United States, and retained as a defendant the attorney general of the United States.

The defendants had changed, the lawyers had changed, most of the claims had changed in some fashion, and even the magistrate assigned to the case had changed six months earlier, when the case's previous magistrate retired.

It should come as no surprise that law journal articles and similar writings about the case often refer to its separate complaints as *Bishop I* and *Bishop II*.

In a case that spanned a decade, it's a wonder that no principal players *died* before it was resolved.

That happened in some marriage-equality cases around the country – one half of a plaintiff couple would die while waiting on a court to allow them to marry.

Over the years, we became Facebook friends with many of these other plaintiffs in what could only be described as a really, really tiny niche group. But our uniqueness also meant that we felt it a lot more intensely when a death or some other "case-threatening tragedy" occurred.

Even though people routinely thank us effusively

for "what we did" and for our sacrifices, one of the biggest risks that most people don't realize we and the other unmarried plaintiffs took was in delaying our own marriages for the sake of the cause.

We, and those other couples, could have traveled to one of the increasing number of marriage-equality states and gotten married there in hopes that our unions would someday be recognized by our own states and the federal government.

But that would have ended our roles in our cases, since we were seeking the right to marry rather than recognition of existing marriages. Other plaintiffs, such as Gay and Sue, were pursuing the recognition aspect, and someone had to remain to demand the right to marry.

Those couples who took that chance and lost – they lost *everything*. Beyond the obvious and universal myriad ways in which losing a spouse can be utterly devastating, those couples also forfeited any future possibility of whatever meager government benefits and rights might have become available to them.

They lost their standing as plaintiffs in a marriage-equality lawsuit that would play a role in bringing down the walls of injustice. They might have lost their right to decide burial plans for their spouse, or they might have lost their home to uncompassionate biological relatives of their dead partner.

And they lost their right, forever, to call that person their legal spouse.

All of those things we said for all those years that we were trying to fix? We and the other unmarried plaintiffs intentionally risked all of those things for that chance to fix them for good. And when a plaintiff died, it really hit home.

In early discussions about the case, one of the key questions Don Holladay had for Mary and me was whether we had ever attempted to obtain a marriage license. He thought our having done so would be necessary if we were to show actual harm.

In fact, we had applied for a marriage license, just about five months earlier, on a Friday the 13th, the day before Valentine's Day.

Part of our newfound relationship with Oklahomans for Equality meant that our appearances as plaintiffs in the case were increasing. Toby thought it was a travesty that so many people – even LGBT people – were unaware of our case, and he never missed an opportunity to shine a spotlight on our efforts.

As such, when he was planning to take a group of same-sex couples to the Tulsa County Courthouse to apply for marriage licenses, he knew that Mary and I should take part. Although no one was under any illusion that licenses would be issued, the idea was to draw attention to the fact that our relationships were treated unequally under the law.

For Toby, this bit of "civil disobedience" carried its own risk.

In those days, Toby was president of the board of directors of Oklahomans for Equality, not its full-time, paid executive director, as he has been since August 2010. OkEq was his volunteer gig; his day job was being the appeals clerk in the Tulsa County Court Clerk's Office. His boss was Sally Howe Smith, who would become our defendant.

Toby had mitigated the risk some – he had taken off work that day so no one could say he was acting on government time, and he had told Sally in advance that we would all be coming in. She was understanding, and the heads up gave her time to prepare.

Toby has said she wanted to be the one to have to refuse to issue the licenses so that one of her deputy clerks didn't have to be the bad guy, noting that some of the couples were her personal friends.

Despite all the precautions, though, Toby was always aware of the potential personal jeopardy.

Six to eight couples participated that day, and as each couple approached the counter and asked for a marriage license application, Sally politely denied the request and gave us photocopies of the laws under which she was doing so.

She was friendly and sympathetic. We didn't have a bad word to say about the experience. Of course, neither she nor we knew then what was to come.

Although our case had had precious little media coverage up to that point, the media did cover the marriage-license event.

The Tulsa World's federal court reporter – the same one who years later officially broke the news of Judge Kern's ruling to us – wrote a nice story that, while focusing on other couples, provided a good synopsis of our case and its status at the time.

This photo of Tulsa County Court Clerk Sally Howe Smith denying us a marriage license on Feb. 13, 2009, was the only official record of our attempt to get a license – and that's how we helped prove that we had standing to file suit. Courtesy

And even though the published photographs were of other participants, the Tulsa World's chief photographer, Tom Gilbert, stopped by Mary's desk to drop off a glossy print of the photo that was snapped of us while we were talking with Sally at the counter, clearly showing all three of our faces.

We didn't know it then, but it was made of gold.

Five months later, sitting in Don's living room, when we told him we had, indeed, sought a marriage license, he immediately began to fret over how we would *prove* that we had; because we hadn't been issued a license, there would be no official record of the attempt.

Oh, there is, we told him. His eyes lit up as we relayed the story about the mass license application and the Tulsa World photographer's picture of us, and that yes, we still had the print.

That photo became an official exhibit in the case, our proof that we had standing to sue over having been denied a marriage license.

CHAPTER TEN:
THE LONG WAIT

Flurries of filings, responses, and responses to the responses followed the submission of our amended complaint, and, as can happen with court cases, activity then came to a standstill.

Once again, life returned to a routine where the lawsuit was sometimes little more than an afterthought. One notable exception came in October 2009, when Mary and I attended the National Equality March in Washington, D.C.

A group of about 30 people from the Tulsa area went, and most of them were strangers to us, further proof that we weren't exactly ensconced in the LGBTQ community in Tulsa, but that trip went a long way toward changing that. Among others, Toby was with us in Washington, and we got to know him personally in a way we hadn't before.

We had been aching for ways to be activists, something that was already difficult as newspaper editors and even more so when the opportunities were so limited.

Our first trip to Washington, D.C., together was in October 2009, for the National Equality March. We were among a group of about 30 Tulsa-area residents who participated in the event, which drew tens of thousands of LGBT people and our allies to the nation's capital.

Courtesy

The feeling of marching with tens of thousands of LGBTQ people and allies down Pennsylvania Avenue, past the White House, toward the Capitol, was indescribable.

Listening to speakers on the steps of the Capitol – including renowned LGBT activist Cleve Jones, who had been friends with Harvey Milk; 1st Lt. Dan Choi, an Army veteran who had been discharged under "Don't Ask, Don't Tell"; and entertainer Lady Gaga – was inspiring.

And feeling like we were a part of something so big and so important was life-affirming. It helped make up for – at least a little bit – the erratic pace of our lawsuit.

Eventually, a "docket hearing" was scheduled for Aug. 31, 2011, more than two years after Don and James had taken over the case. A docket hearing apparently is the courtroom equivalent of watching paint dry – court officials and lawyers for both sides compare their calendars and debate what steps need to happen and when.

Still this was going to be the first time in the nearly seven years since our case was first filed that actual humans were going to stand in a courtroom and discuss it. We wouldn't have missed it for the world.

And sure enough, the most exciting moment was when the court official said aloud, "In the case of *Bishop v. United States* ... ." We had seen that phrase written on lots of documents in seven years, but we'd never heard it spoken, and when we did, we instinctively sat up a little straighter. We didn't know then that we would set foot in a courtroom in connection with our case only one other time and that it would be in Colorado, not Oklahoma.

At that hearing, the case was put on a docket for a trial in May 2012, and the lawyers began preparing their arguments. But before that date arrived, defense lawyers asked the court to suspend the trial schedule.

They knew that a same-sex marriage case – *United States v. Windsor* – was headed for the Supreme Court, and apparently they thought the high court's eventual ruling in that case might make the *Bishop* case a moot point. The judge agreed to suspend the schedule, and the waiting game was on again.

When the Supreme Court issued its *Windsor* ruling in June 2013, it made part of our case – the DOMA challenge – moot, but it stopped short of ruling on the larger question. The *Windsor* ruling required the federal government to recognize same-sex marriages, but it said nothing about whether states had to marry same-sex couples or recognize their legal out-of-state marriages.

On one hand, we were celebrating for Sue and Gay, whose legal marriage would now be recognized at least by the federal government, but we also understood that in Oklahoma, they were still strangers under the law, and that was, simply, unacceptable. So we knew we must press on.

At that point, we could see nothing that would have prevented our case from progressing, but instead, nothing seemed to be happening.

As summer turned to fall, four more states – New Jersey, Hawaii, Illinois and New Mexico – became marriage-equality states, bringing to about 20 the number of states to do so. (Pinning down the precise number was always difficult; sometimes laws were enacted or court rulings were issued at one time but the effective date would be different, maybe even in another calendar year. Other times, court rulings were appealed, or lawsuits were filed over legislative actions. In some cases, couples could continue to marry; other times, the issuing of licenses to same-sex couples was suspended.)

Our lawyers filed a notice with the court in late October that basically said to the judge, "*Windsor* (and cases from several other states that have been resolved since *Windsor* and which relied on *Windsor*) gives you all the information you need to rule in our case. Please do so."

Don had raised the possibility of such a filing with us four plaintiffs, cautioning us that it was a bit extraordinary. It's never a good idea to anger your judge, and such a filing could be seen as nagging, he told us.

But we were growing increasingly impatient, and Don was, too, so we encouraged the filing. Surely this will do the trick, we thought, but we were wrong, and we continued to be dismayed by the silence from the court.

By December, Mary was telling anyone who would listen, "All I want for Christmas is a ruling!"

Five days before Christmas, a federal judge in Utah did issue a ruling striking down that state's same-sex marriage ban, and unlike the cases from other states in which rulings had been piling up, this one would have a direct effect on our case. This was a ruling from a federal court, which gave it a direct path to the Supreme Court.

Except for California, where the situation had become hopelessly complicated by the Prop 8 election, all of the other state cases to that point had been settled via legislative action or a state court ruling.

On top of being a federal court ruling, the Utah decision came from a state that is in the same appellate circuit as Oklahoma – the 10th Circuit.

We will admit it – we were jealous. We had been

fighting this fight for nine years at that point, and the Utah case, *Kitchen v. Herbert*, had been filed only nine months earlier, on March 25, 2013, two days before the Supreme Court held oral arguments in the *Windsor* case. Yet those plaintiffs now had a ruling.

Also, all of the rulings from other states seemed to us simply to add to the mountain of evidence Judge Kern had to work with in fashioning a ruling in our case. But the ruling in the Utah case, in effect, would let him off the hook if he wanted it to.

If he wanted to avoid being the judge who sent a same-sex marriage case on a trajectory to the nation's highest court, this was his out. He could continue to sit on our case in perpetuity, and Utah, it appeared, or some other state's case, would leapfrog ours.

Now let me be clear – we have no idea what Judge Kern's thoughts were at the time, and I would not presume to put words in his mouth. Although we have become acquainted with him since our case was resolved, he's a very private man, and we know little of what he was thinking or whether he even considered such notions. But to our nonlawyer minds, it felt like a chance to change the world was slipping from our grasp.

Many of our experiences with a decadelong civil rights lawsuit presented opportunities for personal growth, although we rarely talked about those deep experiences publicly. This was one of those times.

When we filed the lawsuit in 2004, we saw the issue in terms of (a) wanting to get married, and (b) wanting to right wrongs, but I don't think we understood – and therefore weren't focused on – how much the LGBTQ world would be changed by achieving that measure of equality; just how much taller we would walk as a result of shedding even some of the discrimination we faced regularly.

By late 2013, in the wake of the *Windsor* ruling, we understood that we were potentially on the cusp of something big, and we had come to want a role in it.

In many late-night talks after the Utah ruling, we had to remind ourselves that whether it was the Utah case, our case, or some other case altogether, the bottom line was about rectifying inequality. Change was all but certain to come, and we were going to benefit from that.

In a flash, the year was ending and a new one was beginning. We greeted 2014 with a better attitude, opting not to be so impatient and to go with the flow, confident that we as a country were closing in on the prize, whenever and however it would come to be.

In fact, I completed a New Year's resolution on New Year's Day. For months, friends had been suggesting that we start a Facebook page for the lawsuit.

Mary and I had been remarking about the hundreds of friend requests we were getting on our personal pages as a result of heightened media interest in our case, and while you can never have too many friends, we had begun to notice that we were losing track of our "real-life" friends' posts.

So I created a Facebook page titled Oklahoma

Marriage Equality Lawsuit and promptly started building an audience. Ultimately, I'm not sure we achieved our intent; most people who wanted to keep up with news about the case liked the page but also still sent us individual friend requests!

Still, I couldn't have known on that New Year's Day, sitting home alone and bored while Mary was at work at the newspaper, how fortuitous my creation of that simple Facebook page was going to be 13 days later, when life, as committed gay couples in Oklahoma knew it, would change forever.

CHAPTER ELEVEN:
THE 10TH CIRCUIT

E ven before Judge Kern's ruling in our case was issued on Jan. 14, the new year was starting out busy.

Although only 45 years old at the time, I had cataract surgery on one eye on Jan. 6 and on the second eye on Jan. 13. I'd had Lasik surgery in 2000, so I understood the importance of following strictly the seemingly insane regimen of multiple, frequent eye drops both before and after such a procedure. The first surgery came and went just fine, and the procedure on the second eye was similarly without complication.

But just barely 24 hours later, when we were thrust into a whirlwind of media interviews, Facebook and text messages, and way too many happy tears, I quickly forgot about all those eye drops.

Fortunately, my sister, Jan, and a couple of friends were aware of my situation, and at the rally that night at Oklahomans for Equality, every time I made eye contact with them, they mimicked holding a bottle

Gay and Sue (from right) speak to the crowd at a hastily put-together rally at the Dennis R. Neill Equality Center in Tulsa just a couple of hours after Tulsa federal Judge Terence Kern issued his ruling in our marriage-equality case on Jan. 14, 2014. Courtesy/Oklahomans for Equality

of eye drops up to their faces or mouthed the words "eye drops" to me.

I would think, "I don't have time!" And then I would reach in my pocket for the eye drops and put them in my eye.

I laugh now at how that scenario became something of a metaphor for the following weeks, months and even years of our lives.

Based on the previous nine-plus years of the lawsuit, we expected to have a few really busy days right after Judge Kern's ruling and then fall back into our regular, ordinary lives until the next big development.

Such was not the case this time, however. The media interviews didn't stop. Even though we were journalists, we had no idea just how many smaller and niche publications existed, or that so many of them would want to talk to us! The requests for those interviews were joined by multiple requests for speaking engagements, and then there was the job of keeping up with the case itself.

For most of the next year, it seemed like we simply moved from one appointment or obligation to the next. It felt like we cleaned house only when a reporter was coming over and did laundry only out of necessity.

One day I posted on Facebook that we had run out of coffee more than a week earlier and hadn't had time to get to the store to buy more. I was looking only for sympathy, but friends we'd never met immediately started offering to pick up some coffee and bring it over.

In fact, Mary's longtime friend Phylece LeVally, who lives in Washington, D.C., shipped us some coffee beans! We have always known we were surrounded by good people, but the Great Coffee Crisis of 2014 just drove home that point.

Still, we managed to keep our four cats at the time fed, medicated and with a clean litterbox. Daphne, one of the first two cats we had adopted as a couple nearly 17 years earlier, died four days after Judge Kern's ruling, but her death was not a result of neglect; she had lived for the past 12 years with diabetes and increasing health complications, and we're sure she held on just long enough to see us victorious.

And in a sure sign that we were living in a state of

denial, we took in three baby squirrels and five baby raccoons that spring and summer.

As licensed wildlife rehabilitators, it had always been the injured and orphaned animals that brought chaos to our largely mundane lives each spring; this time, it was the wildlife who were having to go with the flow.

For our part, we learned to do telephone interviews while bottle-feeding baby raccoons, and other rehabbers "babysat" for us from time to time.

Years earlier, on at least one occasion, the lawsuit had taken a back seat to the critters, however.

Late one Sunday night – or early one Monday morning, to be truthful – in August 2011, Mary and I sat feverishly completing draft affidavits that our lawyers had asked us to write.

We had said we'd finish them over the weekend, and since we hadn't yet been to bed, it was still the weekend in our eyes. When we were done, Mary emailed them to the lawyers with a quick note that said:

"Don and James,

"Our affidavit drafts are attached. If we haven't addressed things you want us to, just let us know.

"Thanks for your patience with us. We got new baby raccoons last Sunday, so last week was especially busy for us.

"Mary and Sharon"

As I read her note, which she had copied me on, I began to chuckle, realizing that we had never told the lawyers about our wildlife avocation. So I replied to Mary's email, copying Don and James:

"Wish I could have been a fly on the wall to see Don's and James' faces when they read, 'We got new baby raccoons last Sunday ... .' "

When we awoke later that day, we had Don's typically dry yet hilarious reply:

"From: Don Holladay Monday, August 15, 2011 8:35 AM

"To: Baldwin, Sharon; Bishop, Mary

"Cc: III James E. Warner

"Subject: RE: our affidavits

"I have not read or opened the attachments yet. I was sitting staring at the raccoon sentence when I saw that Sharon had sent a later email. I guessed it might clarify the raccoon remark. It did not.

"In 40 years, I have never before been counsel in a same gender marriage case or had clients with baby raccoons. This is getting exciting."

Much like how we prioritized the raccoons in that instance, we typically tried to be good employees and prioritize our jobs. Although we both still worked full time, our jobs seemed like an afterthought at times.

We will always be so grateful to our supervisors and higher editors at the Tulsa World who basically just "ran with it" during that time.

Always before, we had been conscientious about scheduling vacation days plenty in advance, but three times in 2014 – all three times when court decisions came down in our case – we either just didn't show up for work or left soon after we got there.

We were in communication with the newsroom, of course; they knew *why* we weren't there. But if the editors were ever truly annoyed about making accommodations for us, they never showed it, and our gratitude is beyond measure.

At the root of all that pandemonium, however, was always the case.

Literally 48 hours after Judge Kern's ruling came down, lawyers for Tulsa County Court Clerk Sally Howe Smith filed an appeal of our victory with the 10th U.S. Circuit Court of Appeals in Denver.

As Don and James began preparing for that leg of the fight, Don approached the four of us plaintiffs about bringing on an additional lawyer, one with 10th Circuit and Supreme Court experience. He recommended OU law professor Joseph "Joe" Thai, whom we happily welcomed to our team.

For the next six or eight weeks, it felt like there was a development in the case every few days. After the Court Clerk's Office filed its appeal, its lawyers then filed a request for the case to be put on the fast track.

The Utah case, whose ruling had come 25 days before ours, had been similarly appealed to the 10th Circuit, and parties on both sides of our case were hoping to catch up to it.

The defense lawyers in our case also asked to have the same three-judge panel that would hear the Utah case hear our case, as well; asked for the cases to be heard simultaneously; and asked for the two cases to be allowed to submit the same amicus, or "friend of the court," briefs in support of the similar arguments.

We agreed with all the defense requests, and the 10th Circuit agreed to all of them except the simultaneous hearing. Instead, the court scheduled oral arguments in the Utah case for April 10 and the Oklahoma case for a week later, on April 17.

While Don, James and Joe worked day and night on the multiple briefs the court requested, Sue, Gay, Mary and I got to work raising money to pay for all three lawyers and all four of us plaintiffs to travel to Denver for the oral arguments.

We decided early on that we also should send Don to Denver to hear the oral arguments in the Utah case, since the judges would be the same and most of the arguments would be the same.

Fundraising was something we had focused on quite a bit early in the case because we assumed it would take a lot of money, but few people knew about us or the case then, and income was only moderate. Then, as the case dragged on, expenses were rare, and not really wanting a large stockpile of cash with no obvious purpose, we eased up on our efforts.

With such momentum on our side after the ruling, raising the additional funds for the Denver trip was fairly easy, and we began making our travel plans. My sister, Jan, and our good friend Cheryl Judkins paid their own way to go along with us, as did Don's wife, Kay.

Our little entourage stayed in a hotel less than a

Oklahoma's marriage-equality dream team on the steps of the Byron White U.S. Courthouse in Denver on April 17, 2014, after oral arguments before the 10th U.S. Circuit Court of Appeals. Top row, left to right: James Warner III, Don Holladay and Joseph Thai. Bottom row, left to right: Sue Barton, Gay Phillips, Sharon Baldwin and Mary Bishop. Courtesy

block from the courthouse the night before the arguments, and that's when we saw up close for the first time the similarity between the superstition of baseball players and lawyers. Baseball players are known for having lucky socks. Lawyers have lucky ties. Baseball players get in their zone before the big game. So do lawyers. Ours wouldn't even eat breakfast with us at the hotel on the morning of the oral arguments!

Before we knew it, the big moment had arrived.

We went into the Byron White U.S. Courthouse, through security, and into a maze of hallways before being led to the front row of seats in a surprisingly small courtroom.

I looked around, silently telling myself: "You'll want to remember this. All of this – the pale yellow walls, the high ceiling, the dental molding."

This was only the second time for Mary and me to be in a courtroom in relation to our case, and for Gay and Sue, who had been out of town during the Tulsa docket hearing, it was the first. We didn't know then that it also would be the last; we still had our sights set on the Supreme Court at that point.

There were more lawyers in the room than any-one else. A few journalists sat back in the gallery, and Jan and Cheryl sat behind us. Behind them were friends Leslie and Steve Penrose, who had witnessed Gay and Sue's marriage in Canada.

When the judges entered the courtroom, I was briefly overwhelmed at the enormity of it all. Some-times life just isn't believable. How did *we* get *here*?

Quickly, though, we plaintiffs were struck by something else. The three judges – one white, one black, one Hispanic – looked so much more like our three lawyers – one white, one black, one Asian – than like the dozen or so cookie-cutter young white men sitting at the defense table on behalf of the Alli-ance Defending Freedom, the private, Christian-right legal organization to which then-Tulsa County District Attorney Tim Harris had outsourced the court clerk's defense against our lawsuit.

We know judges don't pay attention to such things in deciding cases, but we thought the similarity couldn't hurt.

Our "home-grown" lawyers were already accustomed to looking like David facing Goliath.

Early in the case, opposing counsel in the DOMA part of our challenge had come from the U.S. Department of Justice. Later, private attorneys – working at taxpayer expense – had entered the case on behalf of the Bipartisan Legal Advisory Group after U.S. Attorney General Eric Holder announced in February 2011 that the Department of Justice would no longer defend DOMA.

Holder and President Barack Obama had come to the conclusion that the law was unconstitutional, but Republicans in the U.S. House of Representatives, acting through the inappropriately named Bipartisan Legal Advisory Group, were determined to continue battling the lawsuits, including ours, that had arisen in the marriage-equality fight.

But just as the Department of Justice had bowed out previously, BLAG had withdrawn from the fight after the *Windsor* ruling left its case in ruins.

All of that legal wrangling was just so much clutter in the background as we sat there in that courtroom and listened quietly while lawyers for the Alliance Defending Freedom described our relationships as lacking legitimate purpose and depth and argued that second-class citizenship was good enough for us, citing procreation and the Bible as evidence.

We knew it was coming, though, and we were

Attorney James Campbell of the Alliance Defending Freedom speaks to the media on April 27, 2014, after oral arguments in *Bishop v. Smith* before the 10th U.S. Circuit Court of Appeals in Denver. The Tulsa County District Attorney's Office had outsourced the court clerk's defense to the ADF, an anti-gay Christian-right legal organization. Courtesy

prepared. We had been reading such comments for years from state lawmakers, the mayor of our city and even the president of the United States, as well as in court filings. Nothing the defense lawyers said suggested to us that they had any argument except the same old worn-out ones.

Don addressed the court on our behalf, but no clock could convince us that he was afforded the same block of time. Perhaps his time just *seemed* to go by faster because we agreed with his arguments.

And then, as quickly as it began, it was over. The judges left the courtroom, the lawyers shook hands, and we all filed out into the hallway, feeling confident and relieved – until I looked out a window and saw a bank of a half-dozen or so television cameras and eight or 10 reporters we didn't know waiting on us to come out and talk to them.

At least in Oklahoma, we were familiar with the journalists. I shouldn't have worried, though. Once before the cameras, we four plaintiffs did what we always did – made the case for why our relationships should be treated equally under the law.

CHAPTER TWELVE: THE BIG DANCE

After our whirlwind 32-hour trip to Denver for the oral arguments, life quickly returned to normal. Well, at least to our new normal – days filled with animal care and nights filled with newspapering, with mornings punctuated by the occasional interview or appearance on behalf of the lawsuit, all wrapped up in the "court ruling waiting game" to which we had become so accustomed.

One major change was quickly on the horizon, though. After 20 years and nine months at the Tulsa World – my only full-time professional journalism job since I graduated from college – I decided to call it quits.

The reasons are many and complex, but two stood out above all the others – keeping up with the lawsuit and related activities was becoming increasingly difficult with us both working full time, and we knew that we wanted one of us to write a book about our experiences with the case.

As it happened, the newspaper industry in general

was going through some growing pains at the time (still is) that made it more logical for me to be the one to step away. And the Tulsa World was making some technology-related changes that, to me, were a beacon on a hill saying, "Now is the time."

I've heard it said that leaving longtime employment can be as emotionally wrenching as a death in the family, and I believe it.

After more than two decades on the copy desk, I had long assumed that I would be the person turning off the lights in the newsroom on my way out the door at the end of the last day of the World/world. And I worked with some of the best people you could ever hope to know. So leaving was difficult, to say the least.

Then again, I had a new purpose, and I was eager to start a new chapter, so to speak. Some 2½ years later, I still miss the people. But it has been exciting to find my voice about not only LGBTQ rights but about a multitude of issues that matter to me. As much as journalists typically love being journalists – we newspaper folk joke about having ink, not blood, in our veins – being able to have and express an opinion is really freeing!

I wasn't forming too many opinions in mid-2014, though, other than those about the glacial pace of judges and courts.

When the 10th Circuit issued a ruling June 25 in the Utah case – 2-to-1 in favor of marriage equality – we felt renewed confidence that we would win, and we thought surely our ruling would come down the next day, if not the same day. The cases were so very similar; didn't they know how to copy and paste? Apparently not.

We not only didn't get our ruling the same day, but we didn't get it the same week. We didn't even get it the same month. We remembered that just half a year earlier Mary had been begging for a district court ruling for Christmas, and we hoped we wouldn't, in another half a year at Christmastime, still be waiting for an appeals court ruling.

Fortunately, the 10th Circuit judges gave us our gift on July 18, affirming 2-to-1 Judge Kern's ruling that Oklahoma's ban on same-sex marriage was unconstitutional.

Truthfully, that's what we expected. Especially after the Utah ruling, we'd have been shocked if the judges had gone against us. But a win is a win, and it calls for a celebration, so Oklahomans for Equality put the finishing touches on a victory rally that had been in the works for weeks.

Although the gathering had essentially the same trappings of our first victory celebration just six months earlier, it felt different to Mary and me.

Even though we had anticipated Judge Kern's ruling literally for years, it had caught us off guard, and much of the celebration and frenzied joy that came in its wake had felt almost two-dimensional. Of course we believed Kern's ruling would be appealed and that our fight would go on, but for that day in January 2014, we were just living in that amazing moment.

Second verse same as the first? Not exactly. At the rally at the Dennis R. Neill Equality Center after the 10th Circuit affirmed our ruling, we celebrated, but our minds were on the business ahead. Courtesy

On the day and evening of the 10th Circuit's decision, though, our thoughts were already 1,200 miles away, at the U.S. Supreme Court. We believed without a doubt that the 10th Circuit's ruling would be appealed. We knew that marriage equality cases from four or five other states were already at some point on the journey from circuit court victory to possible review by the Supreme Court. We wanted to be there, too.

Thus began a multiweek strategy session that made the effort leading up to the 10th Circuit look like child's play.

Within three weeks of the appellate ruling, on Aug. 6, the Alliance Defending Freedom had filed its request with the Supreme Court for review of the case. We had known of the group's intention to do so and were already working on a similar filing, but the ADF's request – formally called a petition for a writ of certiorari – started a stopwatch, and the first response brief deadline was only a month away.

Besides the lawyers' obvious work, discussions were going on behind the scenes about whether we needed to bring on an additional attorney.

Since the earliest days of the lawsuit, when our case was rebuffed by the national groups and then again in 2009 when we were needing new counsel, we four plaintiffs had resisted any alliance with national organizations or, frankly, non-Oklahomans. So when Don, James and Joe told us we needed to consider adding a fourth lawyer, a Supreme Court "specialist," we were hesitant.

For starters, we were so impressed with our legal team that we couldn't believe they weren't up to the challenge. Plus, we felt a bit like we would be betraying them by essentially saying, "You got us this far, but now we want the big guns."

On top of everything else, the "big gun" they proposed was Jeffrey "Jeff" Fisher, the co-director of the Supreme Court Litigation Clinic at Stanford University. The closest thing Jeff had to Oklahoma ties was having grown up in Leawood, Kan., a suburb of Kansas City.

I think the lawyers were surprised that we had to be talked into this, but while it's true that we four plaintiffs are all stubborn and opinionated, it's also true that we are typically reasonable. Once they convinced us of the need – "*No one* goes to the Supreme Court without a specialist; we didn't come this far to lose at the last step." – it was pretty easy to convince us that Jeff was the guy for us.

Jeff and Joe had both clerked for Supreme Court Justice John Paul Stevens, and by this point in his career, Jeff had argued more than 20 cases before the Supreme Court. Articles we found when we looked him up online routinely called him such things as "the elite of the elite." We were sufficiently impressed and decided that as a neighboring state, Kansas was practically Oklahoma.

Ironically enough, at the same time these discussions were happening, we received communication from Evan Wolfson of Freedom to Marry, one of the national groups that had rebuffed us years before, indicating that Freedom to Marry was reaching out to the cases most likely to be before the Supreme Court to offer assistance with communication, messaging or anything else we needed.

He noted that there might be lingering hard feelings but was hopeful that we could overcome them for the greater good.

Don brought the offer to us, and we politely said thanks but no thanks. Much in the way we felt about not giving up on our "local" lawyers, we felt that as two newspaper editors who had the backing of Oklahomans for Equality, we were capable of handling our own messaging. Don replied to Evan that although we would not work against Freedom to Marry, neither were we interested in aligning with it or any national group.

To illustrate his point, he noted that Freedom to Marry had recently begun a campaign to try to get the Alliance Defending Freedom to drop its appeal of the Oklahoma case. Yet we did not *want* the appeal dropped; we very much wanted the Supreme Court to take on and decide the marriage equality issue, and we wanted to be a part of that.

To his credit, Evan replied that the campaign to get ADF to drop its appeal would stop immediately. He understood our approach and acted accordingly. We appreciated that.

Even as our legal team was changing, the case itself was beginning to look a bit different, as well. Although nearly everyone remembers our lawsuit as having secured victories from two federal courts, the fact is that's only partly true.

Our case had always had two parts – Mary and I were suing for the right to marry legally in Oklahoma, and Gay and Sue were suing Oklahoma to make it recognize their legal marriage(s) from elsewhere. Judge Kern had held in January 2014 that the Tulsa County Court Clerk's Office had no official capacity to recognize already existing marriages and that Sue and Gay therefore lacked standing to challenge Section 2 of the federal Defense of Marriage Act.

The judge noted that they "have played an important role in the overall legal process leading to invalidation of Section 3 of DOMA" and praised them and the attorneys "for their foresight, courage, and perseverance."

We appealed that decision to the 10th Circuit at the same time our victory on the primary marriage issue was appealed, and the 10th Circuit affirmed Judge Kern's ruling on that part, as well. Now the question was whether we wanted to appeal that part of the ruling to the Supreme Court.

Our lawyers argued that appealing that issue might be the complication the justices would fall back on to reject our case and take other, "cleaner" cases. Conversely, they said, if the Supreme Court made marriage equality the law of the land, the recognition issue would be a moot point. So we agreed not to pursue an appeal on that part of the case.

In the most technical sense of the word, that meant Sue and Gay were no longer plaintiffs in the case going forward. But that technicality was never a point of contention for Mary and me.

As far as we were concerned, we had started the case with Gay and Sue, and we were going to finish it with Gay and Sue. For the remainder of the case, Gay and Sue continued to be as involved in the decision-making, the press conferences and the celebrating as we were, and we wouldn't have had it any other way.

Besides, we needed their input as much as the lawyers'. With each successive step in the case, the timeframe got tighter and the decisions had to be made more quickly. We relied on our "team" a great deal during those crazy days. Indeed, in an email among the lawyers and plaintiffs on the first anniversary of Judge Kern's ruling, Don reflected: "Little did we realize that we were getting on a slow rollercoaster, with a very fast last curve in the track."

The lawyers were always so wonderful to the four of us plaintiffs. In that same anniversary email, Don wrote: "Little did James and I realize what 4 incredible clients we had taken on. All your attorneys agree it was an honor to represent you."

But I doubt that's what the lawyers were thinking when I emailed them in mid-August and said: "Justice Sotomayor is speaking Sept. 10 at the University of Tulsa. Mary and I have been invited to a private reception in her honor. Can we go and just not introduce ourselves? Can we even go at all?"

The reply from Don was apologetic if firm:

"Our recommendation is not to put yourself in the room. You are the plaintiffs in the biggest case you will ever be in. We need 4 votes for your case to be selected. Your names will be already known by Sept. 10th. Murphy's Law is designed for these situations."

To emphasize his point, he added: "P.S. Your attorneys do not want to worry for two hours on a Wed. night."

It was difficult to hear that; we desperately wanted

to go. Yet we really did understand his point. Everyone in the city would expect us to be there, and that is precisely why we could not be. The quickest way to scuttle our case would have been for some well-meaning person to introduce us to Supreme Court Justice Sonia Sotomayor, who then likely would have recused herself from the high court's decision on whether to take our case.

Just to be safe, I didn't even leave the house that night.

CHAPTER THIRTEEN:
THE WEDDING

The summer of 2014 reminded us in some ways of that summer a decade before, with lawyers working furiously on our behalf in this fight for marriage equality. But in most ways, it was reminiscent because of its differences, not its similarities.

In 2004, no one knew of our quiet, determined labors amid that toxic environment of hate speech and homophobia. A decade later, much of the world knew exactly what we were working on – and much of it supported us! The momentum was definitely on our side, if not for our outright goal of marriage equality, at least for our belief that it was time for the Supreme Court to decide the matter for the nation.

Three weeks after lawyers for the Tulsa County court clerk filed their request for Supreme Court review, Jeff filed a brief from our side, also asking the court to take our case. We filed a little more than a week before our Sept. 5 deadline, hoping, perhaps, for style points for eagerness.

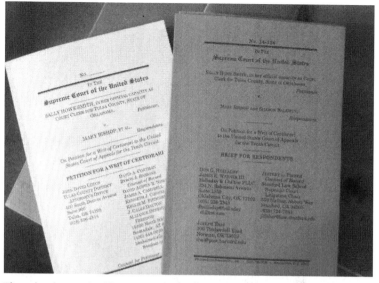

These books are the filings to the Supreme Court in our case, called "petitions for writ of certiorari." The high court doesn't believe in electronic filing; all filings are by bound book in the Supreme Court's own font. The book on the left contains the court clerk's petition plus an appendix that has the district court's complete ruling and the appellate court's complete ruling. The book on the right is our response. Photo by Sharon Bishop-Baldwin

Several cases from other states and circuits were right there with us competing for that coveted Supreme Court review, and we wanted to use every possible advantage.

But as evidence that the integral parties weren't the only ones with a stake in the matter, the attorneys general of 17 states, including Oklahoma, filed a brief on Sept. 6 asking the Supreme Court to answer the question: Does the U.S. Constitution include a right to same-sex marriage? The brief asked the high court to take up the Oklahoma and Utah cases, noting an "astounding" 89 lawsuits ongoing across the nation challenging same-sex marriage bans.

"There are scores of cases requiring thousands of hours to litigate the same legal question presented" in the two states' petitions, the filing stated. "These cases are divisive and costly. ... Once resolved, the legal issues presented in the Utah and Oklahoma petitions are well positioned to provide the necessary guidance to the other states with traditional marriage laws."

With the top lawyers from a third of the states in the nation begging the Supreme Court to take our case, we were feeling like we might have a shot.

As you can imagine, much of the prognosticating about what the high court will do takes place behind the scenes. Although Jeff was good to tell us what information could be considered for public consumption, I think we were programmed at that point to be tight-lipped. Still, it was difficult on occasion to listen to some of our lawyer friends try to discern what the court would do without interjecting what our camp's philosophy was. It was usually much easier just to steer the conversation away from the Supreme Court and on to something more mundane, such as baby raccoons.

According to Jeff, the court was expected to issue its first batch of orders granting certiorari on Oct 2. The next scheduled date for the release of such orders was expected to be Oct. 14, then Oct. 20. Jeff expected to hear something on one of the latter two dates, not the former. He cautioned us that the court would issue a long list of denials on Oct. 6, and we were hoping not to be on that list, of course.

Jeff intimated that most court-watchers were guessing that the justices would take "Utah plus one" and then set the two cases for one hour each of argument. Although there was no overwhelming consensus on which other case in this scenario the court would pick, Jeff said, many observers thought we had a good chance.

Mary and I awoke early the morning of Thursday, Oct. 2, not really expecting to hear anything but wanting to be prepared in case we did. We knew that whether the court took our case or not, when the justices made an announcement, we'd be expected to respond to the media immediately.

As anticipated, the court did nothing with the seven marriage cases before it that day, and even though we knew we could relax for the next four days, doing so was physically impossible. Mary and I spent a lot of time that weekend sitting around the house staring off into space, running through the possible outcomes in our minds as though thinking it through one more time would end in some different, more-confident place.

I think there's an adage that essentially calls that the definition of insanity. I would say that's an apt description of us in those days.

The morning of Monday, Oct. 6, was different, though. We set an alarm to wake up early, although we fully expected not to hear anything about the marriage cases. Perhaps we should have allowed ourselves to believe more strongly that we could end up in the "losers' bracket" and thus be ready to respond, but when the alarm buzzed, I hit snooze instead of hitting the floor.

Two minutes later, I received a text message from our friend Paul Allen saying the court was denying all of the marriage cases. *Then* our feet hit the floor.

Chaos ensued. Which order of business takes priority? Whom do we call first? Which of the four lawyers? Or Gay and Sue? Or Jan? Or Toby? Or our parents? Or Paul Tyrrell, the Tulsa World city editor, to whom we had promised complete access?

Jeff was actually arguing a case before the Supreme Court that afternoon, and we knew he wasn't reachable, so we called Don and Joe. The question on everyone's lips was, "What now?" And at some point, in very short order, Mary or I said something to the effect of "Well, I guess we're getting married today. Right? Can we?"

As Don and Joe set about finding out, Mary and I turned our attention to the media. Paul asked how fast we could be ready for a reporter and photographer to ring our doorbell. We hadn't showered yet, we said. "You better hurry," he said, "because I'll have them headed that way soon."

Personal hygiene was interspersed with conversations with Don and Joe, as well as Toby, who was planning a rally at the Equality Center at a minimum and thinking about plans for our likely wedding that day as well as all the others he would be involved with to some degree.

The "wedding-day" question took a bit of figuring out. We knew that the Supreme Court's decision not to review the case meant the 10th Circuit ruling in our favor was now law. But the 10th Circuit judges had stayed their ruling, and the stay would need to be lifted.

Unfortunately, because of the time difference, the Denver-based court wasn't open for another half-hour or so.

When it did open, the court officials there said they didn't think their stay was the one that needed to be lifted; they thought it was Judge Kern's original stay that was at issue.

Although we've never been able to confirm this, we were told that the then-semi-retired Tulsa judge reportedly was tracked down on a golf course in California, and the stay was soon lifted. We finally knew about 10 a.m. that we'd be getting married that day.

With little to no time for that shocking news to set in, we talked with Toby to start planning a midafternoon press conference at the Equality Center. We let Tulsa World photographer John Clanton film Mary looking through her closet for something to wear – we had thought we'd be June brides after a Supreme Court ruling in 2015, and we hadn't bought wedding attire yet!

We made arrangements with Kevin Flowers, a friend of Mary's from her youth who still lived in Ada, where her mother lived, to bring Fern to Tulsa for the wedding.

At one point, Toby called to say that we needed to get to the courthouse to get our license. A line of other same-sex couples who wanted licenses was forming, but they were waiting on us to get the first license.

I think that was the first time we shed tears that day. How in the world could people be so generous? It was their wedding day, too, yet they were thinking of us. We were overwhelmed with gratitude.

In the same call, we nailed down that we wanted to get married on the steps of the Tulsa County Courthouse, and we tentatively planned the wedding for 5 p.m. Toby said he would get to work on making sure that could happen, and we learned later that he called County Commissioner Karen Keith, who assured him that it was as good as done.

Worried that we wouldn't be able to find a parking place when we went to the courthouse to get our license, Toby told us to go to the Equality Center, where someone would drive us over and drop us off.

As we drove downtown on the Broken Arrow Expressway, it dawned on us that marriage licenses cost money, and we had no cash. Do they take credit cards, we wondered aloud? Who knew? Not us. We decided that if they didn't, we could probably take up a collection on the spot and repay everyone later.

At the Equality Center, we piled into a car with Lucas Green, who worked for Oklahomans for Equality, and his partner, Spencer Brown, as well as Dylan Goforth, the Tulsa World reporter who shadowed us for much of the day, and we headed to the courthouse. As the escalator rose to the second floor, we saw a television camera. And then another, and another, and by the time we became visible to them, cheers and applause broke out from the line of couples waiting for their licenses. The place was a madhouse! But it was a sea of smiles and happy tears, and we felt like we were with family.

Toby and Oklahomans for Equality board member Mike Redman, who is a friend and a lawyer, met us outside the Court Clerk's Office and escorted us to the counter, where a friendly, professional employee helped us complete the application process under the glare of the media lights. For the record, I was able to pay with my debit card, so we didn't have to pass the hat.

We did, however, have to declare at the time of application what our married names were going to be. Fortunately, that decision had already been made – before we had ever met. As a child, I got allergy shots three times a week, and my doctor's receptionist and wife always signed me in. One day, she signed me in as Sharon Bishop. "Marj!" I said. "You know my name!" Bewildered by her error, Marj replied, "Well, you're probably just going to marry a man named Bishop someday." Close, Marj. Close.

From that point on, she signed me in as Sharon Bishop-Baldwin. And that is how we knew, all those years later, which name would come first in our new, joined moniker.

We showed off our hard-won license to the media and were turning to leave the office when we realized that a gay couple standing next to us was getting their license, the second one issued to a same-sex couple. We introduced ourselves to Billy Owens and

As we showed off our hard-won marriage license to the journalists who were present, Billy Owens and Josh McCormick (lower left) were getting the second marriage license ever issued to a same-sex couple in Tulsa County.
Courtesy/Jarrel Wade

Josh McCormick and exchanged congratulations, and we told them how special it was that they had waited for us to go first.

Billy and Josh might have beaten us to the "altar" that day – getting married only an hour or so after securing their license – but because of them, we got the first marriage license ever issued to a same-sex couple in Tulsa County.

Lucas and Spencer handed us off at that point to then-OkEq board President Angela Sivadon, who took us and Dylan the few blocks to the State Office Building to meet with Oklahoma Court of Civil Appeals Judge Jane Wiseman, who had agreed only a couple of hours earlier – when Toby called her on our behalf to ask her – to perform our wedding ceremony.

During the drive over, we were going over some

of the details of the afternoon press conference and evening rally that would take place at the Equality Center. As we were getting out of the car, Angela said to us, "So, I assume you want a cake?"

"Oh, yeah, I guess we should," we replied.

Angela said she would take care of that and added, "And flowers, too, I imagine?"

"Uhhh ... sure," we said.

"Particular flowers you like?" Angela quizzed. "Colors?"

"We've always liked Stargazer lilies," Mary said, "and pink and purple are our colors."

"Good deal," Angela said.

And that was that.

We learned later that Angela called The Garden Trug, whose owners are longtime members and benefactors of Oklahomans for Equality. They agreed to put a couple of bridal bouquets together and then donated them. The bouquets made us cry again; they were so beautiful and were reminiscent of our commitment ceremony flowers! They were as perfect as anything we could have had, even if we'd had months to plan.

Angela and her then-partner (now wife), Mary Robinson, were calling bakeries to try to find a wedding cake, but most don't have spares sitting around, and one can't be made on short notice. Merritt's Bakery had one wedding cake – ordered by a couple who had called off their wedding at the last moment.

"Perfect," Angela said. "I'll take it." Unfortunately, in the chaos, Angela lost her wallet, so she gave the bakery her OkEq business card and said, "Bill us." They never did.

We laughed later, watching all of the television news reports that showed footage of the rally, including that cake. We imagine some man and woman somewhere in Tulsa watching the news and suddenly exclaiming, "Hey! That was *my* cake!"

With Angela on her way to track down the cake and flowers, we headed upstairs to meet with Judge Wiseman.

For at least two years, I had had a note tucked away on my phone with four or five judges' names on it – "finalists" that we, in consultation with Toby, had decided would be ones we could ask to marry us when the time came.

We wanted a judge instead of a minister for a couple of reasons. First, we'd already had a religious rite; our commitment ceremony had been officiated by a minister. Second, the whole point of our lawsuit was about civil marriage and equality under the *law*. It was important to us to stress that, even in the ceremony.

And as career newspaper editors, we had edited a lot of stories about local judges over the years and had a pretty good idea of whose rulings and opinions lined up with our beliefs and values. Judge Wiseman – or Judge Jane, as we affectionately call her today – was at the top of the list.

In retrospect, it's a miracle that when Toby called her that morning she agreed to marry us. Oklahoma appeals court judges appear before voters on a retention ballot every six years, and Jane was going to be on the ballot in less than a month. If there was a great deal of public backlash against her for marrying us, she could have lost her job.

Beyond that, Judge Wiseman was already having a pretty full day that Oct. 6. She had attended the funeral of a friend that morning, and her first grandchild, a girl, was going to be born to her son and daughter-in-law in New York later that day. So can you throw in a midday historic wedding for good measure? Of course, she said.

We had never met the judge, but she greeted us with her arms outstretched to embrace us and offered cupcakes left over from an earlier office gathering. We were, indeed, starving, having skipped breakfast entirely. But Mary was wearing a white linen suit and mine was lavender linen, and the cupcakes were chocolate. Thanks, but no thanks. No sense in tempting that kind of fate.

Even Dylan, sitting nearby and scribbling notes furiously, didn't partake. I wonder if he might have been a bit nervous, too.

We had brought with us the vows we'd said at our commitment ceremony 14 years earlier, and with just a little effort, we were able to incorporate them into the judge's marriage ceremony script. We thanked her and said we'd see her shortly on the courthouse steps and then raced off to the Equality Center in advance of the press conference.

We knew that at least two of our lawyers, Don and Joe, as well as Gay and Sue would be on hand for the press conference. Unlike the media interviews in Denver, walking into a room filled with reporters and television cameras in Tulsa was almost like a family reunion.

So many of those reporters had interviewed us multiple times that they probably knew our talking points as well as we did, and so it might have surprised them when, on our wedding day, we stood before them and said we were disappointed in the Supreme Court.

Of course we were happy to be marrying within a couple of hours, but what would happen the next time we traveled across state lines into an adjacent state that didn't recognize our legal Oklahoma marriage? We would again be strangers under the law.

No, we said, this might be a great day for us personally, but this is not a great day for the LGBTQ people of the country, who once again have been denied justice. The "patchwork quilt" of marriage laws still existed. And it still wasn't good enough.

We didn't know then that the Supreme Court would grant review to a same-sex marriage case – actually six consolidated cases from four states – 3½ months later. It seems that the justices were looking for a disagreement to solve, and our case and the six others denied that day had all gone the same way, in favor of marriage equality.

In the end, the nationwide ruling came no later than it would have had any of the cases denied Oct. 6 been granted review.

With the press conference checked off, we turned

our attention to the big event just 90 minutes away.

Unbeknownst to us, our friend Cheryl Judkins, who had gone with us to Denver for the 10th Circuit oral arguments, had arranged and paid for – along with her partner, Karen Hendricks, and my sister, Jan – a limousine to take us from the Equality Center to the courthouse for the wedding.

Cheryl had spent more than an hour on the phone trying to find an available limousine; there was a run on them, apparently, because of the Katy Perry concert scheduled for that evening at the BOK Center, just a couple of blocks from the courthouse.

In that moment, as she was telling us this, and as we were joking that Katy Perry should come sing at our wedding, we also were realizing that we had two lawyers and a spouse from out of town, an elderly mother and her escort from out of town, and an elderly father and his wife, none of whom needed to be trying to find a parking space near the already congested courthouse and walking several blocks to the wedding.

So we devised a plan to have the limousine act as a shuttle, taking the "wedding party" the 10 blocks to the courthouse in three trips, with the last trip bringing Sue and Gay and Mary and me.

A television reporter covering the wedding told his audience that evening, "Limo after limo pulled up outside the Tulsa County Courthouse this afternoon … ." We laughed ourselves silly. One limo. Three trips. One unintentionally hoodwinked reporter.

On a day where everything that happened had felt surreal and at least a little stressful, the actual wedding put us oddly at ease.

Despite the flock of journalists, including a handful of television satellite trucks parked nearby – at least one of the local television stations carried the wedding live at the top of its 5 p.m. newscast – we were surrounded by people who loved us and had rooted for us. Our parents were sitting close by. My sister was my "maid of honor" and Toby was Mary's, although the many pictures of him holding her flowers during part of the ceremony have led to the popular belief that he was the flower girl.

We had chosen Jan and Toby on purpose. Jan was my witness at our commitment ceremony in 2000, so her presence these many years later was a nod to that history and also to our continued friendship despite being sisters. Jim Stanton, Mary's grad-school friend from Rhode Island, had been her witness at our commitment ceremony, but it was impossible for him to get from Rhode Island to Oklahoma in the four or five hours that was available.

Besides, over the years, Toby had become such a good friend and had worked as hard for this day as we had. It felt fitting and right that he stand up with us at that amazing moment. Of course, as much as Toby and Jan wiped away tears, you'd have thought they didn't *want* us to get married! But we understood their emotions. We shared them, but our utter glee kept our tears at bay.

Our legal wedding was witnessed by a couple

Having a public wedding on the courthouse steps at 5 p.m. on a weekday, what with rush-hour traffic and a Katy Perry concert set to start in a couple of hours just a few blocks away, was perhaps a little insane, but what a thrill! As we looked out over the large crowd, we saw so many faces of friends and loved ones. Equally moving were the faces of all those strangers who just wanted to be a part of history.

Photos courtesy/ Joseph Thai

hundred people, many of whom we knew, but many of whom we did not. They came because they wanted to be a part of history, and we were so happy they did. Even the few shouts that came from cars passing by on the busy street just steps away were congratulatory and joyful.

My sister, Jan Baldwin (seen in lower photo on previous page over my right shoulder), was my attendant, and Toby Jenkins was Mary's. Jan was my witness at our commitment ceremony in 2000 and had been our "cheerleader in chief" since our marriage fight began. Toby, who is the executive director of Oklahomans for Equality, is our dear friend and LGBT equality compatriot. They both cried more during our wedding than we did.

Courtesy

Oklahomans for Equality had arranged for photographer Steven Michael Hall to photograph the wedding, and we're so thankful for that and for his wonderful pictures, because taking photos was one of the last things on our minds.

That wasn't true for everyone, though. Tulsa photographer LeAnne Williams heard that the wedding was going to take place, and even though she didn't know us, she took the initiative to show up, camera in tow.

Although LeAnne had a space of just a few inches between a couple of spectators through which to shoot, she somehow captured the iconic photo of our wedding, the one on the front cover of this book.

We didn't know of its – or LeAnne's – existence until a couple of days after the wedding, when we received a note from LeAnne with an enclosed CD of the pictures she had shot and an offer to do a formal sitting at a later date, as well as news of her plan to provide her services for free to same-sex couples having small, elopement-style ceremonies for the next month or so.

At the Equality Center that evening after our ceremony, eating "stolen" wedding cake and visiting with friends and loved ones for hours, it felt like an old-fashioned family wedding. Never mind that a lot of the guests were complete strangers.

I've tried many times over the last couple of years to describe what that day was like for us, but I don't think I ever can explain it satisfactorily. I just know this: No matter what happens in our lives from that day forward, no matter how wonderful some event might be, I cannot imagine it being better than our wedding day.

Every person should feel that way about his or her wedding day, and I'm immensely proud to have had at least a small role in ensuring that type of joy for a group of people who largely never expected to have wedding days at all.

We love how the writers, editors, photographers and designers at the Tulsa World chronicled our case from initial ruling (top left) to 10th Circuit ruling (top right) to marriage (bottom left). The Tulsa Beacon? Not so much. See explanation on page 145. Courtesy

CHAPTER FOURTEEN:
THE HONEYMOON

If we thought life would slow down after our legal wedding, we were wrong. Besides the ongoing media interviews, speaking engagements and awards presentations, life was just crazy.

Nineteen days after our wedding, we moved Mary's mother from Ada to a house she had bought in our Broken Arrow neighborhood. She was beginning to need occasional assistance, and living from half an hour to two hours' drive away from either of her children wouldn't work any longer. Now, officially my mother-in-law, she was two minutes away by car.

In previous times, we might not have been so eager to take on caring for an elderly parent, especially one whose issues with our relationship had been challenging. But Fern and Mary had made great progress bridging their differences.

Years earlier, my father had asked me privately what Fern objected to about our relationship. When I explained to him that our differences were rooted in religion, he nodded understandingly and said simply: "Well, the way I see it, I can accept it or I can lose. And I'm not going to lose." My dad isn't much for showing emotion, but in that simple sentence, he had said volumes to me.

And this far down the road, it seemed as if perhaps Fern had reached at least something of the same conclusion. She had told us fairly recently that she no longer believed that being gay was a choice.

The fact that she not only had attended but had participated in our wedding illustrated her progress toward acceptance. After our wedding ceremony, she had visited with Randy Roberts Potts, a gay grandson of evangelist Oral Roberts, whom she admired. She told us that had helped her see that *all* families have gay people in them.

We thought we would appreciate having Fern close, and despite the changes in our "family dynamic" and our schedule, we do.

Less than 24 hours after the big move, singer-songwriter Eric Himan was going to be performing as the opening act for Ani DiFranco at Tulsa's historic Cain's Ballroom as part of a benefit for Tulsa's Woody Guthrie Center.

Eric – who had interviewed us for an article he wrote for The Advocate that serendipitously was published only a day before the Supreme Court's action that led to our wedding – had asked us to come to the show. We were exhausted and really wanted to just stay home and sleep. But Eric is a friend, and he was pretty insistent, so we went.

It wasn't long before we found out why he wanted us there so badly. Eric had written a song about us and performed it live for the first time that night!

"Oklahoma Marriage Equality Song for Mary and Sharon," goes like this:

One day, I'm gonna marry you in Oklahoma
Mary and Sharon said it'd be!
One day, I'm gonna marry you in Oklahoma
Now we have marriage equality!

They said we'd always be in last place
They said we were the reddest of all the red states
But thanks to these activists, we can have our wedded bliss
Thanks for giving us the ultimate wedding gift!

One day, I'm gonna marry you in Oklahoma
Mary and Sharon said it'd be!
One day, I'm gonna marry you in Oklahoma
Now we have marriage equality!

Our governor sees our victory as war
She said Oklahomans voted on this back in 2004
Mary Fallin, you're a jerk; you best start looking for new work
cause we are voting you out November 4th!

One day, I'm gonna marry you in Oklahoma
Mary and Sharon said it'd be! (said it'd be!)
One day, I'm gonna marry you in Oklahoma
Now I have marriage equality!

With that, Eric whipped out his own newly mint-ed marriage license while the crowd cheered. Sadly, Gov. Mary Fallin didn't get voted out Nov. 4; she was re-elected easily, and Eric subsequently changed those lines of the song.

But at least for one night, his dig at an unsupport-ive governor brought the house down.

That midterm election of Nov. 4 was actually turning out to be something of a referendum on the LGBTQ community and its allies, and the founder and publisher of the Tulsa Beacon, a small, weekly, ultra-conservative newspaper, was seemingly trying to be the leader of the opposition.

Charlie Biggs previously had been employed by the Tulsa World, where he oversaw the World's weekly Community World editions. Biggs and the Tulsa World parted ways in 2000 – he says because he "felt a Christian could no longer work in that newsroom" – and he and his wife, Susan Biggs, started the Beacon in April 2001. Biggs reported the Beacon's circulation in May 2012 as "around 2,000."

Neither Mary nor I recall having ever spoken with Charlie Biggs, but he did his best – no doubt unin-tentionally – to make us folk heroes of sorts to many of our friends and followers. In an obvious sign that he continued to hold a grudge against the Tulsa World, the Beacon's front-page headline about Judge Kern's ruling in our favor had been "Judge sides with Tulsa World lesbians."

That phrase – Tulsa World Lesbians – quickly be-came a Facebook hashtag, and some friends were even campaigning for T-shirts (Friends of the Tulsa World Lesbians). One would have thought Biggs might have reconsidered the phrase, but on a story about our ultimate victory and wedding, the headline was "Tulsa World lesbians allowed to marry."

Although we all had many good laughs about the nickname, the Beacon's circulation was so small that we honestly never felt threatened. Still, days after our wedding, when campaign signs that read "No Judge Wiseman No" with a red circle and slash across the judge's name began popping up around town, we were pretty certain we knew why, and we couldn't help but suspect that we knew who was behind it.

Judges are allowed to campaign in Oklahoma, although they typically don't, and they're not allowed to publicly state their political party affiliation, in any case. Because judges don't routinely campaign, it's rare to see organized opposition to a judge on a retention ballot, as Judge Jane was going to be in less than a month.

About the same time the yard signs started showing up, the Beacon began campaigning against the judge, writing:

"As the majority of Oklahomans watched in disgust, Judge Jane Wiseman officiated the first legalized homosexual marriage October 6 and called it a 'joyous occasion.'

"Wiseman is on the Oklahoma Court of Civil Appeals. She jumped into the contentious issue of homosexual marriage because she is an ultra-liberal in a conservative state.

Not long after our Oct. 6 wedding, signs like the one on the left began popping up around town targeting Oklahoma Civil Appeals Court Judge Jane Wiseman, who married us and who would be on a retention ballot less than a month later. We weren't about to let her lose. Neither were our friends and followers, one of whom made the sign on the right and placed it nearby.
Courtesy/Sheila Naifeh

"Wiseman gleefully officiated over the wedding of two Tulsa World lesbians, the first time that two homosexuals were married in this state."

Fresh off our marriage equality victory, though, we weren't about to let the judge who married us be punished at the ballot box for standing on the right side of history. We made it our mission to keep Judge Wiseman in office.

One of our Facebook friends made a "retain Jane" meme that was shared several hundred times in the days leading up to the election. Others took it upon themselves to uphold the Tulsa County ordinance that bans political campaign signs on public property – including public rights of way – and remove those signs that were in violation.

As the returns came in on Election Night and it was obvious that Judge Wiseman not only would be retained but retained by roughly the same vote margin as every other appellate judge on that year's retention ballot, I sent her a congratulatory text message. She replied that she had been prepared for the loss, if it had come to that, but she was glad it hadn't. She also asked me to convey to our supporters how much she appreciated our efforts on her behalf.

We had barely gotten the election behind us when Mary and I took a quick trip to Palo Alto, Calif., to speak at the Stanford University law school.

Jeff, our Supreme Court specialist, had told us when he joined our case that his law students in Stanford's Supreme Court Litigation Clinic would be working with him on it. Then, assuming the court took our case, some of the students would go to Washington with us for the arguments. Finally, when it was all over, we would be invited to the college to speak to the clinic students as well as to the law school in general.

Jeff said he thought getting to know plaintiffs as real people and not just as names on cases was good for the students, and this plan had worked well for him in the past.

The prospect of going to Stanford had excited us at the time, but when the high court declined to review our case, we assumed that the speaking engagement would be off. Instead, Jeff said he thought the civil rights issue raised in our lawsuit was of such importance – and that our case had such a history – that it would be beneficial for us to interact with the students anyway. I can only hope that the students got half as much out of our visit as we did!

We first met with the 12 students in the Supreme Court Litigation Clinic, three or four of whom would have worked on our case and one of whom did work on our petition to the high court. Then we spoke to a bigger audience of about 90 people from across the law school. What a fantastic opportunity it was to put a "human face on the case" for those budding lawyers, any one of whom might very well sit on the Supreme Court someday.

Five days after coming home from Stanford, we finally celebrated our marriage in a more formal fashion with a dinner and reception at the Postoak Lodge in the Osage Hills northwest of downtown Tulsa, not far from the property where we intend to build our dream home someday.

In the early years of the lawsuit, we had always thought that house would probably be built before we gained the right to marry, and we could have the wedding there. I'm not sorry it didn't happen that way, though. The Postoak was a gorgeous reminder of the home in the woods we'll have someday, and as was becoming our custom, we were surrounded by so many loved ones and friends.

We really tried in those weeks after the wedding to regain some semblance of a normal life, but it

About seven weeks after our wedding on the courthouse steps, we celebrated formally one last time with a dinner and reception for family and close friends at the Postoak Lodge northwest of downtown Tulsa.

Courtesy/ Tery DeShong

took time – more than we ever would have imagined. Close friends joked about not wanting to go anywhere with us because we would undoubtedly be recognized by strangers who wanted to thank us and have a picture taken with us, and our friends were usually called into service as photographers.

Truthfully, we never minded one bit, and I don't think our friends really did, either. For us, there was great joy in hearing the stories of these new acquaintances – often tear-filled tales of how they never dreamed they'd actually be allowed to marry; sometimes laughter- and joy-laced stories of hurried weddings the same day as ours. The stories were all different, but they were all beautiful, and we never tired of hearing them.

And on occasion, those outings became just a bit surreal. One evening in early December, we had tickets along with my sister, Jan, and our friends Lana Ambrose, Mer Blackwell, Mary Robinson and Angela Sivadon to see Melissa Etheridge in concert.

Some Facebook acquaintances who were in Melissa's fan club saw our Facebook check-in at the theater, so during their fan club meet-and-greet with her, they told her who we were and asked her to give us a "shout-out" from the stage. Not only did she do so, to great applause from a crowd that included nearly every lesbian in Oklahoma, but the acquaintances then pulled Mary and me up to the edge of the stage. Melissa then came over and handed us one of her guitar picks.

During the next song, still at the edge of the stage, Mary leaned back and shouted in my ear, "Should I give her my necklace?"

The necklace was another one of those crazy things that happened in the wake of the marriage equality victory. A local jewelry maker we had never met – Marcie Robertson Givens – had made each of us a necklace with a charm in the shape of the state of Oklahoma and the message "10.6.14 / love won" on it. She had mailed them to us, and I don't think we had been without them more than once or twice since we received them. We even helped get her set up to sell more of the necklaces at Oklahomans for Equality's Pride Store. We thoroughly loved such a

The charm on the left was made and given to us by Tulsa jewelry maker Marcie Robertson Givens. After the Supreme Court made marriage the law of the land in 2015, she made the one on the right.

Photo by
Mary Bishop-Baldwin

unique remembrance, not only of marriage equality but of our wedding date!

Although I really hated to give away one of the first two of those necklaces, it seemed like the right thing to do. So Mary pulled hers off and held her hand out to get Melissa's attention. When Melissa came close, Mary held out the necklace, and she took it. We were so excited to imagine her looking at it in her dressing room after the show!

Of course, that very evening after we got home, I messaged Marcie and said I needed another necklace, stat. I think Marcie was pretty psyched to realize that Melissa Etheridge was then in possession of a necklace she had made!

As if we needed more evidence that we were living charmed lives, just days after our wedding reception, I was at home working on this book when an email popped up on my screen from "The Office of the Vice President." I immediately thought, "Vice president of *what?*" My heart skipped a beat when I opened the email and saw that it was from the office of *the* vice president – of the United States! Joe Biden himself! Mary and I were being invited to the vice president and Dr. Jill Biden's annual holiday party in about three weeks.

I read the email four or five times and forwarded it to Mary's work email without any additional comment, and then I picked up my phone and called her. "Look at your email," I said when she answered. "Now. Just look." Pause. Then: "Oh my gosh. Oh my gosh! Seriously?"

We immediately set about trying to figure out how this had happened, and it took all of maybe 60 seconds to come up with a hunch that turned out to be true. Gautam Raghavan, who was President Barack Obama's LGBT liaison from 2011 through September 2014, had visited Tulsa twice during that time to work with Oklahomans for Equality on a couple of issues, including implementation of the Affordable Care Act in the LGBTQ community.

Mary and I had met with him during both of those visits, and we were certain that he must have had something to do with the invitation.

Only weeks before, we had received a personal letter of congratulations on our legal marriage from the president and the first lady, Michelle Obama, and Gautam eventually confessed to having arranged for the letter. So the Biden party invitation had his figurative fingerprints all over it, and, indeed, he acknowledged that he had put forth our names when the party planners were looking for notable invitees.

We had never in our lives bought plane tickets,

made hotel reservations and traveled 1,200 miles to go to a party that was scheduled to last 90 minutes, but there was really no question as to whether we would go.

As newspaper editors, we'd also never resembled anything like frequent flyers, but here we were, a week after returning home from Stanford, looking once again at flight schedules.

Just like with the Stanford trip, we knew our marriage would not be recognized for the brief time we were in the state of Texas while in the Dallas-Fort Worth airport.

Unlike for the Stanford trip, though, this time we were also submitting our personal information in advance so the Secret Service could do background checks on us. We worried, half-jokingly, that having initially sued the president of the United States might keep us from getting clearance for the party, but that was a different administration, and apparently we had been forgiven.

We arrived in Washington about 2 p.m., five hours before the party was to start. After a quick bite to eat, a nap and changing into our fancy clothes, we got in a cab and headed for the party at the vice president's residence, on the grounds of the U.S. Naval Observatory.

We and our taxi driver did not share a common language, but it was soon clear to us that he wasn't willing to turn into the vice president's driveway! Somehow, we assured him that we belonged there, and he didn't force us to walk the last several blocks.

Visiting the vice president's home was a major highlight in a year of many major highlights. Courtesy

Once on the property, we showed our IDs twice, dropped off the gift we had taken for the Bidens – an official Oklahoma Christmas ornament, complete with the state bird, the scissor-tailed flycatcher – and waited to enter the residence in a long line that snaked through a couple of warming tents where a

Cocktail napkins imprinted with the vice president's seal were placed around the house. We were sure they were to be taken, and we brought some home as souvenirs for friends.

Photo by Sharon Bishop-Baldwin

Marine Corps ensemble performed holiday music and servers occasionally came around with hors d'oeuvres.

Once inside the residence, the first order of business was photos and a brief chat with the Bidens. We thanked the vice president for his personal support for marriage equality as well as the administration's support, not only for marriage equality but for expanded LGBTQ rights in general.

After the official moment was over, we could relax. We literally knew not one other soul there, but we had grown accustomed to resisting the urge to be wallflowers, so we dived in headfirst and enjoyed the food, the beverages and the company, mostly civil servants in the executive branch.

In fact, some of the great people we met that night managed to get us into the White House the next day to see the Christmas decorations! The White House was beautiful and decorated to the nines, but we didn't get to see the Resident in Chief, who apparently was tucked away in the West Wing easing diplomatic relations with Cuba.

After the tour, we made a mad dash back to the hotel for our belongings and headed to the National Press Club for an interview with Chris Casteel, then The Oklahoman's Washington Bureau correspondent, before scurrying to the airport to catch our flight home.

We were gone from home only 42 hours, but those were some pretty amazing hours!

Most importantly, we were happy to be able to convey to Vice President Biden that his support had meant so much to LGBTQ Oklahomans. Few people ever get an opportunity to visit with a president or vice president, or even state and local officials. It was always a priority for us when we did to speak on behalf of our community and not just ourselves.

CHAPTER FIFTEEN:
THE HAPPILY EVER AFTER

A
ll of our speaking engagements and opportunities to visit with movers and shakers had
certainly allowed us to overcome any butter-
flies we might have ever had, but as I soon learned,
diplomacy is a different animal.

It seemed that politics was often our focus late
that fall and winter, and in a state as deep red as Oklahoma, much of that interaction was with people of
different political persuasions.

Now-former state Rep. Sally Kern spent much of
her tenure in the Oklahoma Legislature making a
name for herself not only state- and nationwide but
even around the globe because of her extreme views
on LGBTQ rights. Sally had hit the peak of notorie-
ty in early 2008, when she said in a speech – secretly
recorded – before a group of Republicans:

"Studies show that no society that has totally embraced homosexuality has lasted more than, you
know, a few decades. So it's the death knell of this
country. I honestly think it's the biggest threat our

nation has, even more so than terrorism or Islam – which I think is a big threat, okay? 'Cause what's happening now is they are going after, in schools, 2-year-olds … . And this stuff is deadly, and it's spreading, and it will destroy our young people. It will destroy this nation!"

Sally's on-the-record antics weren't nearly as laughable; they were downright scary. Her vehemence against the LGBT community via proposed legislation was notorious in Oklahoma. Our only consolation was that her measures were typically so far beyond the parameters of constitutionality that they were either watered down beyond recognition or tossed out entirely before reaching the governor's desk.

In mid-December 2014, with the start of the 2015 legislative session still six weeks away, Mary and I found ourselves at the state Capitol to receive the 2014 Human Rights Award from the Oklahoma Universal Human Rights Alliance. The ceremony was held in the fourth-floor House chambers, and the recipients and spectators alike sat in lawmakers' chairs at the lawmakers' desks.

Afterward, we were milling about on the House floor when some Norman high school students who also had been honored started screaming that they had found Sally's desk. I sat in Sally's chair and put my feet up on her desk, and the students thought it was hilarious. One of them told Mary to stand behind me holding our award, and she did, and the student snapped a photo.

This picture was a hit with friends and followers but turned out to be a good learning experience for me. Courtesy/Rachael Smith

I posted the photo on Facebook – as the fourth of four photos in a collage – and it spread like warm butter on hot bread.

Our friends and followers responded with cheers and joy as though we had planted a giant rainbow flag on top of Mount Bigot, and I'll admit, that's how it felt, too.

One friend commented on the Facebook post of the photo: "Oklahoma's most notorious lesbians are baiting Oklahoma's most notorious legislator. Symmetry and alliteration."

Toby told me later on that he cringed a bit when he saw the picture. His feeling was that as a representative of the LGBTQ community, I needed to be a little better than that. I listened to what he said, but in that moment, I chalked it up to just a difference of opinion. I didn't really see what he saw.

But something changed over the days and weeks that followed, and I came to regret the photo – not because Sally didn't deserve it; she did. She deserved way more than that. Kern, whose 2011 book "The Stoning of Sally Kern: The Liberal Attack on Christian Conservatism – and Why We Must Take a Stand" detailed what she saw as her persecution, was formally reprimanded by her own colleagues that same year for racist and misogynistic comments made on the House floor.

Sally had said during debate about a bill to end affirmative action in Oklahoma:

"Is this just because they're black that they're in prison, or could it be because they didn't want to work hard in school? I taught school for 20 years, and I saw a lot of people of color who didn't want to work as hard. They wanted it given to them."

Later on, she said women are paid less than men because "women usually don't want to work as hard as a man," adding that they'd rather stay home with their family.

Still, Toby had been right. Sally was so wrong about so many things, but being disrespectful wasn't going to gain us any leverage toward proving it. That was a great lesson for me personally, and it couldn't have come at a better time.

As the legislative session got underway just six weeks later, Sally Kern introduced a trifecta of anti-LGBT legislation. Although she wasn't the only Oklahoma lawmaker to take aim at our community, she won the dubious honor of "lawmaker single-handedly proposing the greatest number of anti-LGBT measures."

The first would have barred any state or taxpayer funds from paying for anything related to the recognition or licensure of same-sex marriages. The second was aimed at giving parents the unimpeded right to force their gay children to undergo conversion therapy in an attempt to make them straight. The third would have allowed anyone or any business to discriminate against LGBT people or organizations for any reason or for no reason.

But as I said, Sally Kern was far from the only Oklahoma lawmaker to target the LGBTQ community that session. More than two dozen measures were proposed with the primary and obvious intent of rolling back equal rights where possible and preventing the expansion of equal rights in other areas. Constitutionality clearly was never a concern, and we quickly came to understand that the onslaught was really just an attempt to punish us for the marriage equality victory.

Ultimately, only one of the bills that seemed targeted at us became law. House Bill 1007 allowed clergy members to refuse to marry anyone they didn't want to marry and would give them immunity from lawsuits based on any such refusal. The bill also has the distinction of being the only one we didn't fight – because that right and subsequent immunity are already enshrined in the First Amendment to the U.S. Constitution.

Other victories came early in 2015, too. The city of Tulsa's Fair Housing Ordinance was found during a routine review not to provide protections for LGBTQ Tulsans. Toby and Oklahomans for Equality took the fight to the City Council, but frankly, it wasn't much of a fight. About half a dozen of us addressed councilors about the types of discrimination that we or people we knew had experienced in housing, and we asked them to add sexual orientation, gender identity and gender expression to the ordinance. Eight city councilors, most of them Republicans, sat listening and nodding.

Councilor G.T. Bynum, who would become the city's mayor about a year and a half later, asked one of the most telling questions when he said, "Isn't this kind of a no-brainer?" We thought so. The other councilors apparently thought so, too – the vote was unanimous in our favor.

As we have said all along, Oklahoma truly is the reddest of the red states, but a true map of the state would show a lot of blue smudges, and it was always our experience that Tulsa was one of those spots.

And if legislative and municipal victories weren't enough, it appeared that the LGBT community was going to get a chance with the nation's highest court after all.

The news came down in mid-January that the Supreme Court was, in fact, going to take on the issue of marriage equality during the 2014-15 term. Six cases from four states – Michigan, Ohio, Kentucky and Tennessee – were consolidated into one case that ultimately became known as *Obergefell v. Hodges*.

Many observers found the consolidation worrisome, but we welcomed it, remembering that one of the greatest civil-rights cases in our nation's history – *Brown v. Board of Education* – was a consolidated case. It had combined five cases representing 13 plaintiffs from four states – Kansas, South Carolina, Virginia and Delaware – and Washington, D.C.

We thought the consolidation of the marriage cases meant the justices were truly trying to cover the bases and not render a piecemeal opinion that would extend the patchwork quilt of marriage laws even further.

The high court slated oral arguments in the Obergefell case for April 28 and asked the parties to answer two questions:

1) Does the Fourteenth Amendment require a state to license a marriage between two people of the same sex?

2) Does the Fourteenth Amendment require a state to recognize a marriage between two people of the same sex when their marriage

was lawfully licensed and performed out of state?

And with that, scores of lawyers across the country got to work preparing to help argue the greatest civil-rights issue of a generation.

In Oklahoma, Sue, Gay, Mary and I began hearing talk through our connections with plaintiffs in other marriage cases across the country of burgeoning plans for a reception of some kind for all of us in Washington around the time of the oral arguments in the *Obergefell* case.

Although Freedom to Marry had been recruited by the Key West, Fla., plaintiffs to host and fund the event, many other plaintiffs had feelings similar to ours about the lack of support for our cases from national groups, so there was some debate about the event's promotion and messaging. Freedom to Marry, however, agreed to host and fund a gathering without suggesting to the public or media any greater role than that.

With that settled, the reception was planned for the evening before the Supreme Court oral arguments. We four Oklahoma plaintiffs were once again making travel plans, aware that as we passed through the Dallas airport, we would once again be strangers under the law because Texas did not yet recognize our marriages.

We arrived in Washington the evening before the reception, and Mary and I had another interview the next morning with The Oklahoman's Chris Casteel.

The location of the reception that night had been

Mary, Sharon, Gay and Sue outside the U.S. Supreme Court in Washington, D.C., on April 28, 2015, during the oral arguments in *Obergefell v. Hodges.* Courtesy/Phylece LeVally

kept much like a state secret for fear of a media onslaught, but the event was held in a law office on an upper floor of a downtown office building with floor-to-ceiling windows that provided a stunning view of the Washington Monument.

We heard from Freedom to Marry founder Evan Wolfson and President Obama's senior adviser, Valerie Jarrett, with whom we got to visit, thanks *again* to Gautam Raghavan, who by then was working for the Gill Foundation and was also in attendance.

It was great to meet in person so many of the plaintiffs we had gotten to know on Facebook, but the highlight of the night was just standing back and looking at that room packed with people who had all done exactly what we did, albeit at different times and places and under different circumstances. The energy in that room was something special, and I'll never forget that feeling.

Sue, Gay, Mary and I were up early the next day to meet Phylece LeVally, Mary's college friend from their days at East Central University in Ada. Phylece lives in Washington now, and she joined us for the rally outside the Supreme Court and stored our luggage in her car so we could make a quick dash to the airport after the rally.

Some people – including some of the other plaintiffs – prioritized being in the courtroom during the arguments, even though they would be allowed to remain inside – in the back – for just a few moments. But just like at Best Buy for Black Friday, a line for observers had begun forming the week before, with people setting up camp and others being paid to stand in line as placeholders.

We felt more inclined to stay at the rally outside, listen to the speeches and take in the atmosphere, which was electric. In many ways, it was like Pride – complete with protesters and preachers – except we all were condensed into a much smaller area. The ever-growing list of days I will never forget most assuredly includes this day.

A quick flight back to Oklahoma for a rally that evening at the Equality Center to present a show-and-tell of our trip brought to a close our jam-packed trip to the Supreme Court.

In retrospect, it turned out OK that we were more spectators and less litigants. Equality was the clear winner, regardless of whose name was on the case.

On June 26, 2015, the Supreme Court ruled 5-4 that the Fourteenth Amendment to the U.S. Constitution requires all states to grant marriage licenses to same-sex couples and recognize the marriages of same-sex couples granted in other states. The *Obergefell v. Hodges* decision came on the second anniversary of the *United States v. Windsor* ruling, which struck down Section 3 of the Defense of Marriage Act, and on the 12th anniversary of the *Lawrence v. Texas* ruling, which struck down state sodomy laws.

And in all three cases, the majority opinion was written by the court's familiar swing vote, Justice Anthony Kennedy. In the closing paragraph of the *Obergefell* opinion, Kennedy wrote:

"No union is more profound than marriage, for it embodies the highest ideals of love, fidelity, devotion, sacrifice and family. In forming a marital union, two people become something greater than once they were."

INDEX